WB-D
D

$9

Oriental Rugs

Oriental Rugs

A GUIDE TO IDENTIFYING
AND COLLECTING

Pamela Thomas

Robert Hale • London

A FRIEDMAN GROUP BOOK

Copyright © 1996 by Michael Friedman Publishing Group, Inc.
First published in Great Britain 1996

ISBN 0-7090-5977-9

Robert Hale Limited
Clerkenwell House
45-47 Clerkenwell Green
London EC1R OHT

ORIENTAL RUGS
was prepared and produced by
Michael Friedman Publishing Group, Inc.
15 West 26th Street
New York, New York 10010

Editors: Hallie Einhorn and Stephen Slaybaugh
Art Director: Jeff Batzli
Designer: Andrea Karman
Photography Editor: Colleen A. Branigan

Colour separations by Ocean Graphic International Company Ltd.
Printed in China by Leefung-Asco Printers Ltd.

DEDICATION

To the memory of my grandmother, Sarah Porter Bosworth, and to her great taste.

ACKNOWLEDGMENTS

No book can ever be the work of only one person. Although this book was a great pleasure for me to research and write, its great glamour comes from the rugs themselves and, in the case of this book, from the pictures of the rugs. Many carpet experts, photographers, and institutions are responsible for these marvelous photos.

Specifically, I would like to thank Hossein Montazaran for his invaluable help with the pictures and his generosity in providing useful information not only about his own rugs, but about identifying and collecting Oriental rugs in general. In addition, I greatly appreciate the help of Vickie C. Elson, George Hanassab of Hanassab Oriental Rug Imports, Robert Ouzounian of Persian Rug Company, Philip Garaway of the American Indian Art Gallery, and Jack K. Ouzouian of Artex Rug Gallery and Textiles, all in Los Angeles, for the use of rugs from their collections. I also want to thank Richard Todd for his great help—and great taste—in selecting and photographing the rugs from these various sources.

Certain organizations permitted the use of images of rugs from their collections, including Darwin Bregman Associates, the Rosalie and Mitchell Rudnick Collection, the Museum of Art at the Rhode Island School of Design, the Victoria and Albert Museum in London, and both the InnerAsia Trading Company and FPG International in New York. I am grateful to them all.

Finally, I want to thank Colleen Branigan of the Michael Friedman Publishing Group for her dogged and thorough photo research. Also at the Friedman Group, my original editor Hallie Einhorn was particularly intelligent, meticulous, and thoughtful in her role. She was also extremely patient when I occasionally lagged behind. Steve Slaybaugh arrived to take Hallie's place when she left New York, and he did a marvelous job of picking up his stepchild. And lastly, a word of appreciation to Sharyn Rosart for once again thinking of me.

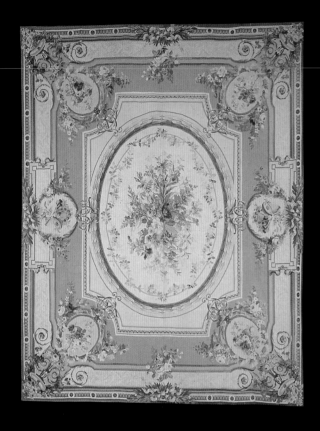

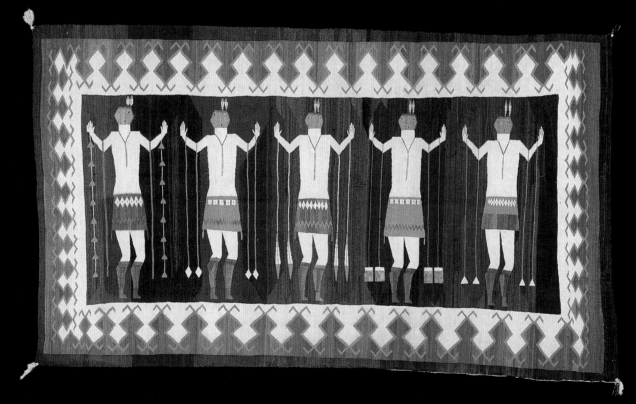

CONTENTS

AN INTRODUCTION

TO ORIENTAL RUGS

A decade ago, shortly after my grandmother's death, my uncle came to visit me bearing a few odds and ends that had been left to me in my grandmother's will. Among them was a large bundle that I recognized immediately, without even unrolling it. It was an Oriental rug that I had seen many times in an upstairs bedroom of my grandmother's house. Although I loved Oriental rugs, at the time I owned only one rather ragged piece, which I had bought at a flea market in New Hampshire for $65.

When I unrolled the precious package, I was surprised to discover that two additional treasures were wrapped within the larger one. The big familiar rug was a nice camel-colored Hamadan that my grandmother had bought during her honeymoon in the Middle East in 1921, while the smallest one was another Hamadan that I had no memory of ever seeing before. But it was the middle-sized one that turned out to be the true treasure, both in sentiment and in value.

I remembered this rug from my childhood when it rested in front of my grandparents' fireplace. My favorite color has always been red, a predilection I shared with my grandfather, and because of this rug's deep ruby coloring, I liked to sit and play with

This is a classic example of an Isfahan rug, considered one of the most beautiful types of Oriental rugs in the world. The multilobed center medallion design, the intricate border, and the finely stitched jewel-like blue, cream, and red colors are typical of these rugs.

my dolls on it for hours when I was a little girl. Much later, after my grandfather died and my grandmother moved to a small apartment, she placed this rug in her entryway. I noticed it with pleasure—

and probably commented on it—nearly every time I visited.

This, too, was a rug my grandmother had bought in Persia in 1921. It is a very finely made Sarouk, and today, almost

*S*hown here are the world's most prominent Oriental rug–producing countries. The so-called "rug belt" normally includes only Islamic nations, not China and the other Far Eastern countries.

....

seventy-five years later, it still shimmers with the jewel-like quality it must have exuded when my grandmother bought it to adorn her first home. I have no idea how much my grandmother paid for this treasure, but according to my local rug dealer, today it is worth about $3,000. However, for me, the Sarouk—and the two far less valuable Hamadans—are priceless.

Many people have similar stories about these magical works of art called "Oriental rugs." Perhaps they own a rug with senti-mental—or financial—value, and they want to know more about their special car-pet. Maybe they have purchased a pretty rug in Iran, Turkey, India, or China and are curious whether they got a "good deal." Or possibly, they have decided that a nice

Oriental would be the ideal solution to creating an attractive focal point in their living room.

Whatever the reason, Oriental rugs are very popular these days, as they have been for centuries. Not only are they beautiful and prized by a broad spectrum of people, but they can be one of the surest financial investments one can make in today's erratic economy.

Oriental rugs are endlessly fascinating. Regardless of whether it is a humble tribal piece from Turkistan or a priceless Isfahan carpet from Iran, each rug has a unique character. If you fall in love with it, you can be certain that it will be among your most prized possessions for the rest of your life.

❶ROMANIA ❷GEORGIA ❸ARMENIA ❹AZERBAIJAN ❺TURKEY ❻TURKMENISTAN ❼AFGHANISTAN ❽IRAN ❾PAKISTAN ❿TIBET ⓫NEPAL ⓬INDIA ⓭CHINA

What Is
an Oriental Rug?

Oriental rugs are handwoven textiles made primarily for the purpose of covering a floor, but they are also used to cover doorways, tables, chairs, and windows; they are often made into pillows, bags, and even saddle covers and tents. Some rug experts, mainly art historians and museum curators, define a "rug" as the textile as it appears when it is removed from the loom—unfinished; and a "carpet" as a finished object, easily identified as a floor covering. Other experts, mainly commercial brokers and dealers, define a "rug" as a small finished piece, about 3 by 5 feet (91 by 152cm) or less, and a "carpet" as a finished piece that is larger than 3 by 5 feet. In North America, a rug is usually referred to as a smaller piece that is used as an accent in a room, and a carpet as a large piece that covers an entire floor. Throughout this book, the two words will be used interchangeably.

There are two basic types of rugs. *Kilims* are woven in a simple manner, like a tapestry, by looping loose, horizontal threads (called *weft* threads) around stationary, vertical threads (called *warp* threads) to create patterns. These rugs are also called *flat-weaves*, and are among the oldest known rugs.

The designs used in Oriental rugs from the Middle East and the Far East employ designs based on patterns that have been indigenous to the regions for thousands of years. This unusual Tibetan rug, entitled "Eight Auspicious Symbols," employs Taoist, Buddhist, and Chinese symbols.

....

The so-called pile rugs are more sophisticated handwoven carpets. They are made by knotting hundreds of thousands of threads through the cross-hatched network of warp and weft threads. With the exception of very old or rare kilims, pile rugs are considered the more valuable of the two types, because more work is required to create them.

The relative value of a pile rug is often expressed in the number of knots per square inch (referred to by the cognoscenti as *ksi*). Although some very old and valuable pieces are loosely knotted (made with fewer knots per square inch), the finest rugs have many knots per square inch, usually 200 to 400 for a good rug, and as many as 800 knots for a masterpiece. The more knots per square inch, the clearer the design, and thus, the more valuable the rug.

The elaborate designs used in Oriental rugs and carpets are based on patterns that have been indigenous to regions of the Middle East and Far East for hundreds of years. They include medallions, flowers, animals, and geometric patterns, many of which are thought to have religious or symbolic meaning and usually reflect the rug's place of origin. The complex skills employed in creating the wools and silks, mixing the dyes, and weaving the rugs has been passed down for generations from craftsman to craftsman.

*his Bijar rug employs a strong medallion design on a field of roses, a motif frequently used in rugs made from this village. Bijar rugs are known for their dense weaving, which creates long-wearing carpets.

....

What Makes an Oriental Rug Oriental?

Over the past hundred years or so, we have come to think of the "Orient" as synonymous with the "Far East," particularly China and Japan. However, an older definition of the Orient, perhaps best symbolized by the *Orient Express*, the deluxe nineteenth-century train that ran from Paris to Istanbul, includes any region east of the Mediterranean. Traditional Oriental rugs were and are created in what we now call the Middle East.

The primary, or traditional, rug-making region is known as the "rug belt." This region runs across more than 2,000 miles (3,218km) from Morocco, in North Africa, to western China. Basically, the area encompasses the boundaries of the Islamic world, and the rugs created there reflect the prevailing Islamic religion as well as many other aspects of the culture. Some historians believe the art of rug weaving developed as native peoples

established ways to cope with the climate and terrain. Despite the size of the region, it is relatively uniform in terrain: arid and mountainous with little rain or vegetation. Because of the nature of the land, sheep- and goatherding became a common way to earn a living. Moreover, many sheep-herders were nomadic, and in order to create portable household articles—including a safe dwelling—they learned how to spin yarn and weave necessities.

However, despite the uniformities, the artistic genius evident in many of the rugs emanates from the individual cultural and physical aspects specific to the smaller localities that make up the rug belt. Although the materials and techniques are basically the same, the color and the quality of wool or silk and the intricacies of design vary greatly. A rug from Morocco is as different from a rug

made in Iran as Waterford crystal is from Venetian glass.

Today, we still recognize the rugs of the Middle East as the traditional Oriental rugs. However, as a result of historical developments, especially in the fifteenth, nineteenth, and twentieth centuries, rugs created using Oriental designs and tech-niques have been and continue to be pro-duced in Eastern Europe, England, France, Spain, China, and even in Scandinavia and the Americas. While some of these rugs were purposely adapted from classic Middle Eastern designs, others, such as the French Aubusson carpets and the antique Chinese rugs, are unique and indigenous to their region. Nevertheless, rug dealers—and rug buyers—still consider them to have the same artistic value as fine Persian or Turkish carpets, and therefore they are often sold or auctioned as "Oriental rugs."

Oriental rugs can be used in myriad ways to decorate a room. In this living room, rugs are used as floor and furniture coverings, wall hang-ings, and pillows. Many different styles and colors can be used to create the ultimate effects of warmth and elegance.

This Nepalese rug, woven in a Tibetan design, bears a striking phoenix motif, a well-known Chinese symbol commonly seen in Tibetan and Nepalese rugs.

....

A B i t o f

H i s t o r y

Weaving is one of the oldest crafts known to mankind, possibly because it arose from necessity. No one knows exactly how long rugs have been woven, but the art of weaving is mentioned in both the Old Testament and in Homer's *Iliad*, so it has definitely been a practice for more than two thousand years. In fact, the oldest known Oriental rug in existence, the Pazyryk Rug (sometimes referred to as the Altai Rug) dates back to about 500 B.C.

The Pazyryk Rug, which hangs in the Hermitage Museum in St. Petersburg, was found during the late 1940s by a Russian archaeologist, S. I. Rudenko, in the grave of a Scythian warrior prince. (Like royalty from many cultures, Scythian nobles were buried with their most valued possessions.) Apparently, the grave was robbed not long after the burial. The gold objects and precious stones were taken, but the rug was left behind. By a stroke of providence, the grave was flooded and the rug was frozen, so when it was found, more than two thousand years later, it was remarkably well preserved.

The Pazyryk Rug is a pile carpet, tied with a Ghiordes (Turkish) knot, about 200 knots per inch. (Curiously, other rug fragments found in the same grave were tied with a Senneh knot.) Almost square in shape, it has a central field with a madder or rusty red color and repeat squares of a floral motif. Several different borders surround the field, and within some of the broader borders, elk, horses, and riders are depicted. Some experts believe that the rug is of Persian origin; others, however, believe it was woven by Mongols, who often used animal images.

Much of Oriental rug history involves Mongolian weavers, and a substantial amount of evidence indicates that the earliest rugs were woven by Mongols or peoples of the Mongolian region who moved west. It is also thought by many experts that Mongolians introduced weaving into China and Tibet. Nevertheless, Chinese Oriental rugs enjoyed a history all their own, and the rugs have a unique, subdued, quietly elegant feel to them, which is much different from the colorful jewel-like quality of the Middle Eastern designs.

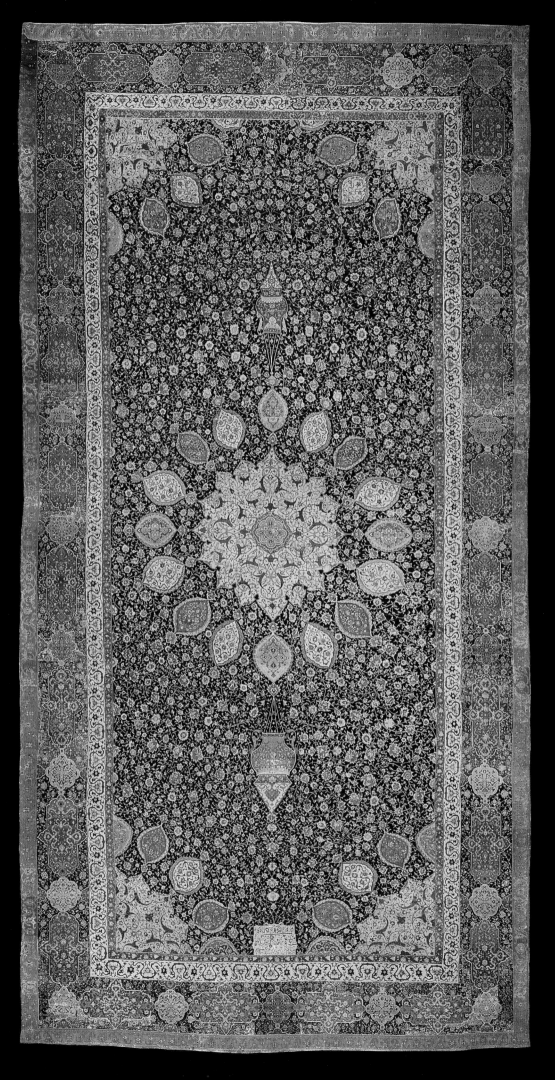

A few other famous rugs are important in rug history. In the sixth century A.D., Chosroes I, a Persian king, ordered a spectacular rug to be made to celebrate his defeat of the Romans and his conquest of Arabia. The rug, known as the Spring Carpet of Chosroes, no longer exists, but records indicate that it was enormous, over 400 feet (122m) long and 100 feet (30m) wide. It was woven with gold and silver and studded with precious jewels. The design was created to imitate a spring garden with paths and colorful flowers so that the king could stroll along it as though he were in the midst of a delightful garden. When Heraclius defeated the king's son, Chosroes II, in A.D. 627, the rug was cut up by the victors for souvenirs.

The Ardebil Rug, which was woven in about 1540, is one of the most famous extant examples of Persian rug making. It was purchased by the Victoria and Albert Museum in London in 1893 for about $4,000, which at the time was considered an outrageous amount to pay for a rug. To make matters worse, it soon became apparent that the rug had been repaired with pieces of a twin, which today hangs in the Los Angeles Museum of Art. The rug, which has a sapphire blue background with a gold medallion design, is made of wool on silk warp and weft threads.

While the Persians were busy producing their most exquisite pieces during the fifteenth and sixteenth centuries, the Europeans were in the midst of the Renaissance. Although eleventh-century Crusaders were probably the first to bring Middle Eastern rugs to Europe, Renaissance explorers, beginning with Marco Polo, were responsible for introducing valuable rugs into European trade. Only royalty, the nobility, and the very rich could afford such rugs, and they had these prized acquisitions proudly displayed in their portraits. (The paintings of King Henry VIII by Hans Holbein include the king's Oriental rugs.) By the sixteenth century, imported carpets had become so fabulously expensive that France's King Henry IV (1553–1610) organized the production of "Oriental" rugs within the boundaries of his nation, thereby spawning the creation of the exquisite Savonnerie and Aubusson carpets.

By the eighteenth century, Oriental rugs had made their way to North America. With industrialization, man-made dyes and mass production rendered rug making less expensive. Nevertheless, although Oriental rugs flooded into Europe and the United States, the best rugs were still available only to the very wealthy. In the late nineteenth century, pioneers and tourists began to make their way to the American West and discovered finely woven rugs fashioned by Native Americans, primarily the Navajo. These rugs have come to be considered as valuable as Middle Eastern and Chinese Orientals.

The art of rug making has continued throughout the twentieth century, not only in the Middle East, but in Europe and America as well. Formed with ancient weaving techniques and materials, but displaying fabulous modern designs, contemporary rugs are being created throughout the world. Paul Klee (and others of the Bauhaus movement), Pablo Picasso, Henri Matisse, and scores of other significant painters have designed rugs of matchless quality.

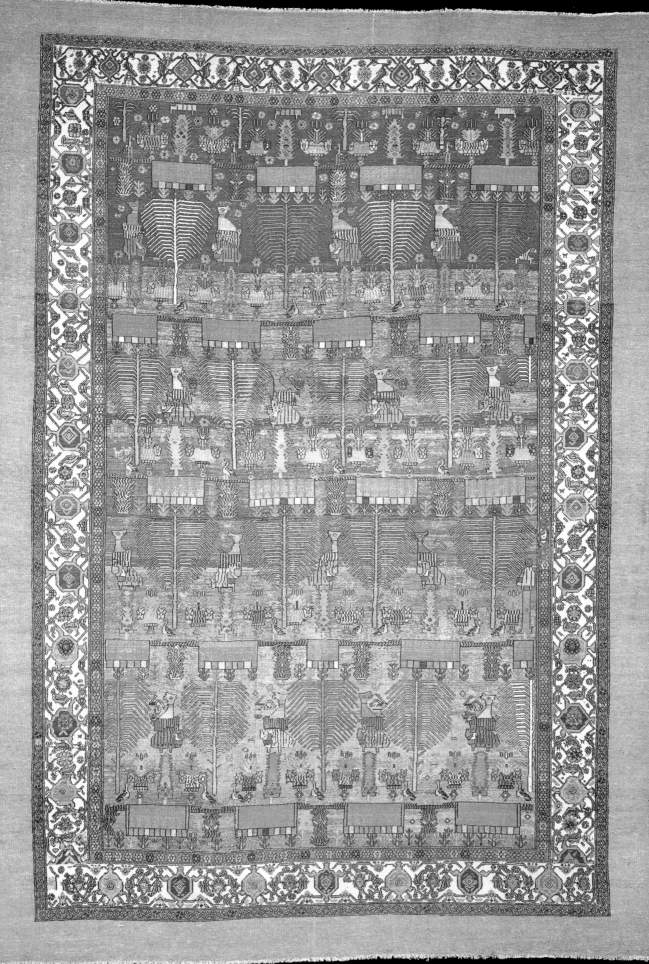

*O*pposite: This Persian Malayer rug is designed in a somewhat unusual repeated panel design using muted earth tones. This type of rug comes from the town of Malayer in Iran, which lies halfway between Hamadan and Arak.

....

*R*ight: While not technically Oriental rugs, Navajo rugs are considered to be as valuable by many dealers and collectors, and are often sold at Oriental rug shops and auctions. The value extends to contemporary rugs, like this work from the Two Gray Hills region of the Navajo reservation, made in the 1940s.

....

Rug Construction

and Color

Regardless of where they are made, all Oriental rugs are woven in much the same way. The weaving process is conducted as follows: the warp threads are attached to the upper and lower beams of a loom so that they run vertically. A strand of colored wool (or silk) is knotted around a pair of warp threads repeatedly across the width of the carpet. The loose ends of the knots, which make up the pile, form the colorful body of the rug. After each row of knots (or sometimes several rows of knots) has been completed, a weft thread is run horizontally through the carpet to secure the knots in place. Kilims, which, do not have pile, are made by weaving colorful weft threads through warp threads in order to create a design. Whether such rugs are woven by Eastern Indians, American Indians, or even French artisans, the process remains the same.

The Weaver's
Tools and
Techniques

The tools needed for rug weaving are quite simple: a loom of some sort; and wool, cotton, or silk to create the rug. With these basic elements, the weaver is able to create exquisite works of art.

Looms

Two basic types of looms are used for weaving rugs: a horizontal loom, which usually rests close to the ground; and a vertical loom, which stands upright. The horizontal loom is the simpler of the two. It is used primarily by nomads and also by some weavers living in small villages. Its beams are held in place by large stakes that have been driven into the ground. Because it is difficult to maintain an even warp tension with this type of loom, the resulting rugs often have irregular sides.

Vertical looms range from simple contraptions to large, complex industrial machines. The simplest type of vertical

loom is also used in villages. With this device, the weaver sits on a plank that is raised as the weaving progresses to enable her to position herself directly in front of the area of the carpet on which she is working. The length of the carpet is usually as long as the distance between the upper and lower beams of the loom.

Vertical looms can be more complicated. With the so-called Tabors loom, the warp threads form a continuous loop around the upper and lower beams. As the rug is woven, it is lowered around the lower beam and up the back of the loom. The "roller beam" loom is even more sophisticated. As the weaving progresses, the rug is rolled up around the bottom beam. As a result, the rug can be any length.

With the simpler looms, only one weaver works at the loom on the rug. More complicated looms allow two or more weavers to work simultaneously on one large carpet.

Preparing the Wool

After a sheep is shorn, the wool is thoroughly washed to get rid of dirt and grease. Then it is dried and sorted. Next the wool is combed in order to align the fibers so that when spun, a strong yarn is produced. Finally, the wool is carded to prepare it for spinning. Carding is accomplished by repeatedly brushing the wool with two wooden paddles (called cards) that contain slanted metal teeth until the fibers are untangled, soft, and fuzzy. After carding, the wool is ready to be spun.

The spinning of wool is an ancient process that has been practiced for hundreds of years. During spinning, the fibers are drawn out and twisted together, either by hand or by machine. Wool fibers that are spun together form one strand of yarn; two or more of these strands are twisted together to form plied yarn.

Hand-spinning is performed with a spindle, which is composed of a wooden dowel and a crosspiece or disk. The spinner wraps the fibers around his or her wrist or arm, attaches them to the spindle, and then pulls and twists them, creating a continuous thread or yarn. Spinning can also be done on a spinning wheel, which basically consists of a spindle attached to a rotating wheel.

The direction that the yarn is twisted is important, since this aspect can affect the strength of the yarn. The yarn can be twisted either clockwise in a right-hand direction, called S-spun, or counterclockwise in a left-hand direction, called Z-spun. The same terminology is used for the plying of the yarns. For the best yarn, the strands should be plied in the opposite direction from which they are spun. For example, a warp thread that consists of three strands of S-spun wool should be Z-plied.

Harvesting Silk

Silk comes from the incredibly long single thread with which the silkworm spins its cocoon. (A single thread can measure more than 1 mile [1.6km] in length.) The finest silk comes from the first part of the thread; the coarsest silk (called slub silk) comes from the bits at the base of the cocoon.

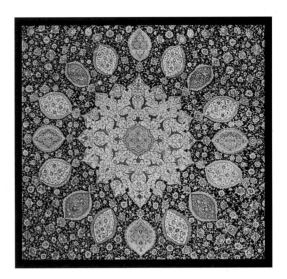

Silkworms are carefully farmed, and when the cocoons are harvested they are boiled and brushed to create the final threads. Although the production of silk originated in China, today it is carried out in Iran and Turkey.

Warp Threads

Attached to the upper and lower beams of the loom, the warp threads form an important basis for the rug's structure, and must therefore be strong. The type, thickness, and color of warp fibers vary from country to country, village to village, and even tribe to tribe.

Wool used for warp threads is spun by hand or machine and then plied. The number of plies varies according to the tradition and style of the weaving center. Goat or camel hair is sometimes woven with the sheep wool, especially in more primitive areas. Cotton, spun either by machine or hand, is also commonly used. Machine-spun cotton warps were introduced in the rug-weaving industry in the mid-nineteenth century, as a result of industrialization. Most are made of Indian cotton spun in England. Machine-spun warps are more uniform strands, generally of five plies or more. Hand-spun warps, on the other hand, are more coarsely spun, with only three or four plies, and tend to be less uniform in width.

Silk, too, is used for warp threads, but to a lesser degree than wool and cotton. Although silk is the strongest warp in relation to its diameter, it is also expensive and refined. As a result, only the finest rugs are woven with silk warps.

W*eft* T*hreads*

A pass of a single weft between two rows of knots is called a "shoot," and the number of shoots used between rows of knots varies depending on the weaver and the weaving area. In some rugs, there may be as many as five weft shoots between two rows of knots.

As with warp threads, cotton, wool, and silk are commonly used, either singly or in such combinations as wool and cotton; wool, cotton, and goat hair; or cotton and silk. Usually used in their natural form, wefts tend to be white, gray, brown, or black. Sometimes, however, they are dyed in a variety of colors, particularly red, pink, or blue.

T*he* K*nots*

Two basic types of knots are used to attach the yarn: the Ghiordes knot (also known as the Turkish knot or symmetrical knot) and the Senneh knot (also known as the Persian or asymmetrical knot). Generally, the Ghiordes knot is used in the western end of the rug belt, and the Persian knot is used in Iran and eastward.

The Ghiordes knot is formed by encircling two warp threads with a strand of

*W*hen worked on a loom, the warp threads, made of cotton or silk, are strung vertically and secured. Then the knots are tied in a row or rows, using the colored wool. The weft threads are woven across the vertical warp threads and tamped down, holding the knots in place.

This young woman is copying a design that she has propped up at eye level. At the moment, she is creating the colored knots.

yarn, and then looping the ends tightly between the two warps. The Persian knot is formed by first encircling one warp thread with a strand of yarn, then winding the strand around another warp, and finally pulling one loose end between the two warps. The other loose end emerges outside the pair of warps either to the left or to the right.

There is also a third type of knot, called the jufti, which is known in the rug trade as a "double knot" or "false knot." This knot can be either a Ghiordes or Senneh knot that has been wrapped around four instead of two warp threads. Thus, the weaver is making only half the number of knots, thereby decreasing the density of the pile, and weakening both the structure and design of the carpet.

In order to identify the type of knot used, bend the rug horizontally and open the pile. The Ghiordes knot is the easiest to identify; a strand of yarn is visible as it passes over the warp threads.

The Pile

Obviously, the quality of the pile has much to do with the quality of the yarn. The majority of Oriental carpets are woven with wool yarn, the quality of which varies greatly from region to region, as different factors affect texture and color. The best wool is "kurk" wool, which comes from the chests of lambs and is used to create the finest Persian rugs. The poorest-quality wool, sometimes called "dead" wool, is wool that has been removed from butchered sheep, and it is dry and brittle. Sometimes other fibers, such as camel hair or goat hair, are combined with the wool, giving the pile a bristly texture.

Silk threads may be used for pile in the finest rugs, or they can be combined with wool to achieve a certain effect or to accentuate certain parts of the designs. Mercerized cotton, sometimes called "artificial silk," resembles silk in that it has a soft texture and a sheen. Occasionally, mercerized cotton, particularly bright white, is used on pile as a decorative accent in Turkish and Turkoman rugs. Beware, however. Some disreputable dealers occasionally try to pass off cotton as silk, but a close look will show that cotton does not have the softness or luster of silk—or even wool.

End Finishes

In order to remove the carpet from the loom, the warp must be cut. The portion of the cut warps that remains attached to the carpet is known as the fringe. The cut warps or fringes must be finished in a way that prevents the woven knots from coming loose.

The most common methods used to finish off these ends involve either a knotted fringe or a narrow band of kilim with fringe. The kilim may be plain or woven in colors or patterns; sometimes a knotted pile or embroidery is added. Some rugs have fringe at only one end. In such cases, the opposite end may be simply turned under and sewn, or a simple band of kilim weaving may be added.

Side Finishes

The side edges of a rug may be secured in a number of different ways. Sometimes a simple selvage is formed by weaving several of the warp threads with the weft threads. Or the selvage can be reinforced by adding an overcasting stitch, using one or two colors of yarn, along the entire side of the rug. In some regions, a side cord is sewn onto the edges of the carpet after the carpet has been completed.

Cutting and "Shaving"

As the rug is being woven, the tufts are left hanging, and therefore it is difficult to see the design. Occasionally, as the weaver is working, she will trim them to about 2 inches (5cm) in length, and the design will begin to emerge. When the rug is completed and taken off the loom, it is taken to a master shearer, who "shaves" the rug to create the pile. Needless to say, this process rerquires the work of a skilled professional, for the length of the pile must be even. If the shearer slips, he may ruin months of dedicated labor.

The Basics of Dyeing

One of the most outstanding characteristics of Oriental rugs is the astonishing range of colors used to create the designs. The dyeing of the fibers used to create rugs is a delicate process that varies according to the dyestuff used and the colors desired.

Requiring a great deal of skill and precision, this intricate process is considered an art form. In fact, the master dyer (who invariably is male) is a revered and sometimes mysterious figure in the village. In many towns and tribes, his advice as a wise man is sought on a range of subjects, particularly those concerning herbs, and his secrets concerning the dyes are guarded and carefully passed down from generation to generation, father to son.

Before the dyeing process can begin, the wool must be properly prepared. After it has been spun, it must be cleaned again so that the dyes can penetrate the fibers. The wool is then treated with a chemical mordant to fix the dye. Common mordants are

Opposite: Men are responsible for dyeing the wool, and the master dyer (top, left) is always revered and sometimes considered almost a mystical person in the village. It is not unusual to see hundreds of skeins of wool hung out to dry in many Middle Eastern villages (top, right). The colors are created by artisans (bottom) in many different ways, depending upon the color desired. Regardless of the method, the color is always rich.

....

alum, iron, chrome, and tin. Depending upon the mordant used, the color of the dye can be altered.

The actual dyeing process is as follows: after the yarn is cleaned and treated, the skeins of wool are submerged into a dye bath, which is a solution of water and dye. The bath is brought to a boil, and the wool is carefully stirred to ensure uniform coloring. After the dyeing has been completed, the wool is hung to dry in the sun. Once dry, it is ready for weaving. Silk and cotton yarns are dyed in much the same way, using the same kinds of dyes.

The actual creation of the dyes is a complicated process. Two basic types of dyes are used: natural dyes and synthetic dyes.

Natural Dyes

Natural dyestuffs are derived from insects or plants, the latter being the prevalent source. The most common dyes made from plants include madder, which creates a brownish red color and comes from the madder plant; indigo, which results in a clear blue hue and comes from the leaves of the indigo plant; weld, which comes from the weld plant and makes a yellow or gold color; pomegranate, which produces an orange hue; onion, which creates a yellow or copper color; and walnut, oak, and other nuts, which create shades of brown. Some insects frequently used are the cochineal, which produces a red hue, and Dactylopius coccus cacti, which creates yellow.

The colors produced by the plants or insects can change drastically, depending upon the mordant used to fix the dye. For example, an onionskin dye combined with alum yields a golden yellow, but the same dye fixed with chrome produces a copper color.

Natural dyes are the oldest dyestuffs used, and they can create beautiful colors and carpets. Depending upon the quality of the dyes, a rug colored with natural dyes can be remarkably valuable.

Synthetic Dyes

Many people consider rugs colored with synthetic dyes to be of poor quality. But this generalization does not always hold true; rather, the quality of such a rug depends upon the kind of synthetic dye used.

The first synthetic dye was fabricated in 1856 by William Henry Perkins in London. Known as aniline dye, it was applied directly to the wool in an alkaline solution. Initially, the dye seemed to be an effective means of creating bright colors relatively easily and cheaply. However, it turned out that the colors were not fast; they bled when washed and faded dramatically when exposed to sunlight.

In the 1870s, another kind of dye was developed, called a direct acid dye, which was applied to wool in an acidic dye bath. Although these dyes did not fade, they did bleed when exposed to water, and they were often harsh in tone. Azo dyes, also of the direct acid variety, were introduced in the late nineteenth century. These proved to be of better quality, though some colors still bled.

In the 1940s, chrome dyes, which require a chromium mordant to fix the color, were developed. When such dyes are used, the wool is treated with potassium dichromate so that it takes the dye more readily and evenly. Still other metal complex dyes were developed that combined the dyestuff and the mordant, creating additional colors. Finally, fiber-reacting dyes were developed in recent years. With these dyes, the color-giving part of the dye molecule binds with a wool molecule, permitting the dye to become a part of the wool's chemical structure. As a result, these dyes are highly colorfast, but expensive.

D y e s
a n d   R u g
Q u a l i t y

The quality of the dye affects the value of a rug in two ways: the shade and intensity of the color itself and the colorfastness. Rugs woven before the 1870s will have been made with natural dyes; rugs woven after the 1870s could have been dyed in one of several ways. The quality of the color will be obvious; that is, it will be attractive or it will be harsh or faded. Colorfastness, on the other hand, will not be readily apparent unless the rug is already badly faded. Buyers can test color by lightly rubbing the rug with a white handkerchief moistened with saliva.

Sometimes a variation in tone, known as abrash, is visible in a certain area of the carpet, such as the field. This variation occurs either because the yarn absorbed the dye unevenly or because the yarn used was taken from different dye lots. The abrash can be attractive, giving the carpet a mellow richness, or it can be abrupt and harsh. Again, the fact that the color varies is not the issue; what is important is how the variation in tone has been executed.

W a s h e s

After rugs are woven, they are almost always washed in order to get rid of excess wool and dirt. The simplest, most primitive wash is done by tribal or village craftspeople in local streams. The rugs are then laid in the sun to dry. Strong sun often softens harsh colors.

In more developed areas, some rugs are given chemical washes to soften the colors. A luster wash may also be given to a carpet after the initial chemical wash to give the rug a lustrous sheen. Finally, to create an aged look, various rugs are given an antique wash, a special chemical wash developed to tone down colors and create a drab, muted appearance.

"P a i n t e d" R u g s

During the 1920s and 1930s, many rugs exported from Persia were considered too bright for the North American market. So that they would be more appealing to Americans, these rugs were given not only a chemical wash, but a hand-applied "painting" that darkened the color. (Usually, red carpets received this treatment so that they would become maroon.) This painting process was followed by yet another process to add luster to the carpet. Most Sarouks were "painted" in this manner, as were some Mahals, Hamadans, and even some valuable Isfahans.

*O*pposite: After the weaving process is completed, rugs are washed to clean off excess wool, oil, and dirt. In small villages, rugs are taken to a nearby river or stream, scrubbed vigorously, and then left in the sun to dry. This primitive cleaning method should reassure collectors of the durability of their treasures.

The term "painted" can have both a positive and negative connotation. Many Oriental rugs that have come to be considered valuable antiques, such as the Sarouks, were painted. Like the use of various synthetic dyes, the painting technique does not necessarily affect the value of the rug, unless the process was poorly executed, creating a blotchy appearance.

However, sometimes the term "painted" is used to refer to rugs that have been colored by ink or acrylic paints to hide worn areas. In these cases, the alteration not only lowers the value of the rug; it is unethical.

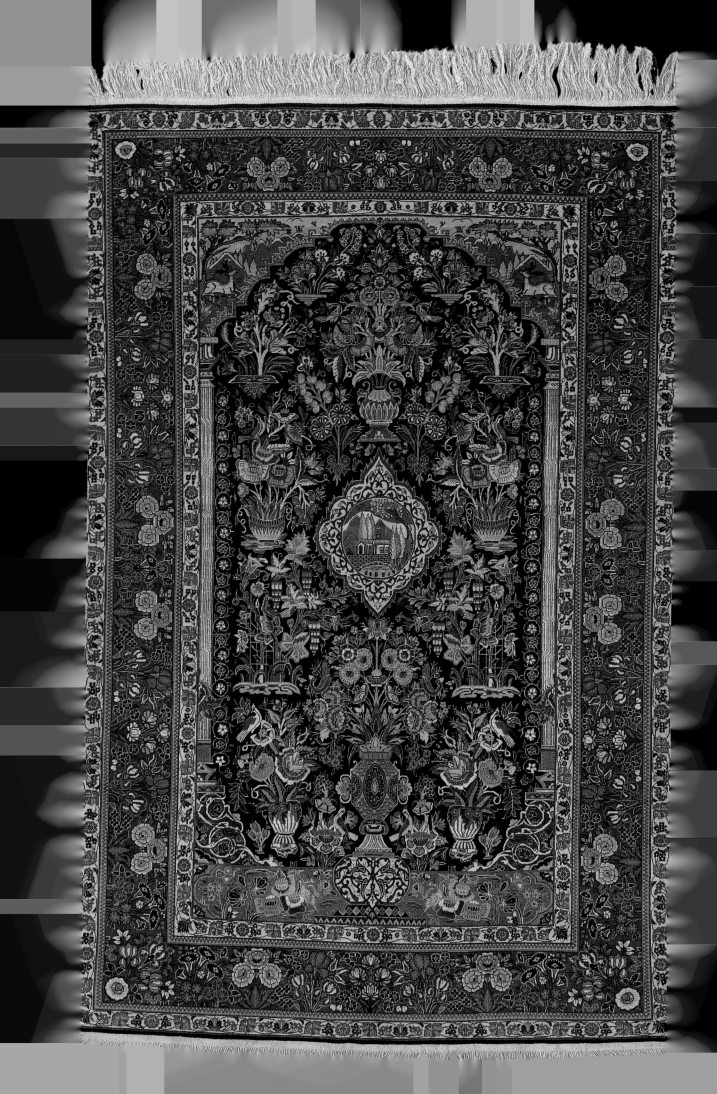

ASPECTS OF

RUG DESIGN

The designs of Oriental rugs, particularly if they are from Turkey or Iran, reflect the village or area where they are made. The basic styles of these designs can be hundreds of years old. Usually a pattern is purchased from the local village artisan (sometimes at great expense), and then a family or a local workshop builds the loom, spins the wool, creates the dyes, and weaves the rug. Even in the smallest villages or among tribal weavers, a designer, who is usually a highly respected artisan, creates a pattern that is purchased by the weaver. In the Middle East, the designer is always male, while the weaver is always female.

Although Oriental rugs come in infinite designs, these designs can be broken down into simple groupings that make identification and discussion much simpler. Rug designs are of two basic types: rectilinear and curvilinear. Rectilinear designs are angular and geometric, while curvilinear designs are flowing, tending to be more intricate and refined. Sometimes rugs combine elements of both styles, although usually the more angular styles are created with fewer knots per square inch, while the curvilinear styles require many more knots to create the rounded edges.

In terms of the overall design, a rug can be divided into two parts: the field and the border. While the field (and the design woven into the field) serves as the focal point of the rug, the border acts as the frame.

This small Nepalese rug, which measures 32 by 44 inches (81 by 112cm), is a classic representation of the rugs woven in the Tibetan region. The floral pattern and the porcelainlike colors exhibit a decidedly Chinese influence.

This classic prayer rug is from Kashmir, India. Prayer rugs are common throughout the Islamic world, particularly in Turkey and Iran. This rug measures 36 by 46 inches (91 by 117cm), a classic size for such rugs, which are designed to be portable. This floral design reflects the Persian influence; indeed, finely woven silk rugs like this one are often mistaken for Persian carpets.

The field composition can be classified into seven basic types: prayer, medallion, repeat motif, allover pattern, open field, panel, and portrait. Within these main categories, the different styles and variations are practically infinite.

Prayer Rugs

Prayer rugs were originally designed as mats to be used during prayer. (The Islamic faith requires praying to Allah several times a day.) Small in size, usually 3 by 5 feet (91 by 152cm), they are easily

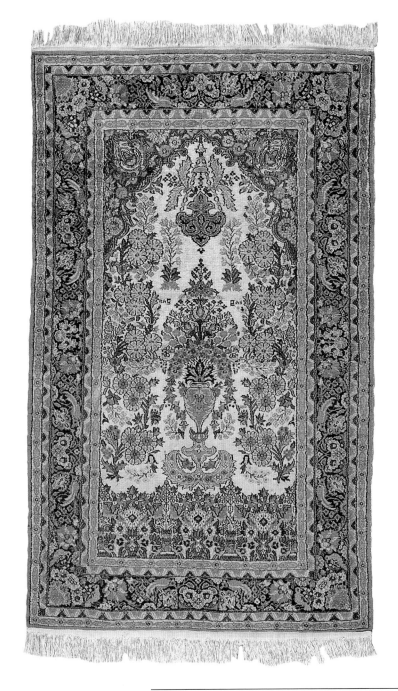

This exquisite prayer rug is a classic Persian, woven in a mille-fleur pattern. The soft blue and yellow colors in this rug are unusual, and the intricate, finely woven flower bursts and borders give it additional value.

portable and ideal for kneeling on. Prayer rugs are woven throughout the Oriental rug world, including such areas as Turkey, Iran, Afghanistan, the Caucasus, and Turkistan, and copies of traditional Persian and Turkish designs are woven in Pakistan, India, China, and Romania.

Prayer rug designs are perhaps the most classic Oriental rug motif. The rugs have a prayer niche (called a *mihrub*) or arch that forms the focal point of the field. Depending on where and how the rug was woven, the arch can be rectilinear or curvi-linear. In some styles, the arch is supported by columns. The area within the arch is called the spandrel and is decorated in patterns reflecting the style of the region of origin. (The term "spandrel" is also used to describe corner designs in some rugs.) Turkish prayer rugs often have a panel at the top or bottom of the field.

Some rugs have multiple niches, called *saphs*. Such rugs are meant for family use, with one niche or saph for each family member. Saphs are commonly woven in Turkistan and Turkey.

*M*edallions

Medallion design rugs have a field that is dominated by a single central medallion or by two or more medallions. In some rugs, medallion motifs are repeated in the corners (spandrels). (In Iran, this medallion and corner design combination is called *lecheck torunj*.) Medallions appear in many styles, sizes, and shapes, including round, oval, geometric, and elongated. The field surrounding the medallion may be open or filled with pattern.

*R*epeat *P*atterns

Repeat pattern rugs are carpets that have a motif that is repeated over and over in the field. The Bukhara rugs of Afghanistan with their repetition of small "guls" is the most familiar example. Other regions produce designs with repeated stripes or medallions.

Allover Pattern

A rug displaying an allover pattern has a feild filled with a variety of motifs that are not repeated or regimented in any way. For example, the feild may depict a hunting design, a garden design, or the classic-tree-of-life design.

Open Field

The open field design is precisely that—an open or empty field containing no motifs or design elements. Chinese rugs are often created with an open field. When the rugs are woven with fine wool that has been exquisitely dyed, the abrash of the open field is especially rich. Often the empty field is surrounded by one or several borders, which can be quite elaborate.

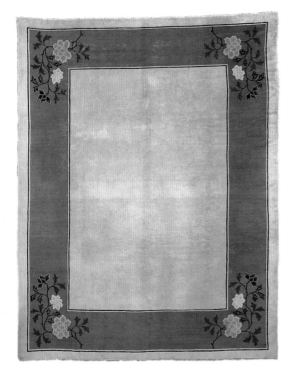

Paneled Designs

Paneled designs are characterized by a series of compartments or panels that can be in the shape of squares, rectangles, or diamonds, and that enclose such design elements as flowers, trees, stars, or small geometric figures. Some experts believe that paneled designs reflect the precious irrigation channels that have been constructed throughout the rug belt to allow for gardening or farming in the arid and inhospitable andscape.

Pictorial

Early pictorial carpets were influenced by European paintings. Such rugs display landscapes, portraits (particularly of kings or important leaders), and sometimes exact replicas of particular works of art. (Atatürk, the father of modern Turkey, was a popular subject.) Contemporary designers often use photographs as the basis of their designs, sometimes depicting leaders like Lenin and John F. Kennedy in black and white. In Afghanistan after the war in 1980, rugs bearing pictures of fighting machines such as tanks and helicopters appeared, often in surprisingly attractive forms.

Smaller Design Elements

While only seven basic styles of designs exist, the smaller and more detailed design elements are almost infinite. For example, a rug with a central medallion may have a great number of rosettes or a paisley pattern filling the basic motif. Or a rug with a repeat pattern may make use of various

Below, left: This classic Chinese carpet features an open field, that is, a complete absence of design in the center of the carpet. Although some Middle Eastern rugs have open fields, this design element is much more common in Chinese rugs.

Opposite: This marvelous Persian rug features an allover pattern. In other words, the field is filled with various, rather haphazard designs, in this case a traditional "tree-of-life" design with flowers, birds, and meandering leaves.

classic motifs known as guls. Many of these elements are considered to have symbolic or religious meaning. Of course, unique design elements can be created by a gifted designer or weaver. However, in the world of rug design, there are hundreds of small design elements that are used frequently and have become classics. Those that are used most often in many different cultures and styles are:

B o t e h (*Paisley*)

This teardrop-shaped or pear-shaped motif is used frequently in Persian, Caucasian, Turkoman, Indian, and Turkish rugs. It is best known to Westerners as a "paisley" motif, since it was the defining motif of wool shawls created in a well-known woolen mill in Paisley, Scotland. The boteh is thought to symbolize fertility or lush growth, which is highly valued in the arid Middle Eastern region.

H e r a t i (*Mahi*)

This design derives its name from the town of Herat (formerly part of Iran but now belonging to Afghanistan), where it originated. It is composed of a single floral head within a diamond framework surrounded by four curling leaves. It is sometimes referred to as the "mahi" or "fish-in-the-pond" motif, which is based on a Persian myth that the world is supported by four swimming fish. There are many variations of this form, but it is usually employed in either an allover design or in a medallion format. It is most commonly found in Persian rugs, although India now produces rugs using classic Persian techniques, including this pattern.

M i n a - K h a n i

This pattern is a variation on the Herati motif. It is composed of repeated floral motifs surrounded by four similar but smaller flowers that are joined by vines to form a diamond shape. It was originally a Persian design, but is now often used in Indian rugs that are woven in the Persian style.

Left, bottom: The boteh design, or paisley pattern, is one of the most common design elements in Oriental rugs. It symbolizes fertility, a highly valued concept in the arid Middle East. *Left, top:* The Herati, or Mahi, pattern is another classic design element. It can be described as a flower surrounded by leaves or a pond surrounded by four fish.

Opposite: The Mina-Khani pattern is another floral motif made up of a large central flower surrounded by four smaller flowers. This pattern is often found in antique Bijars and Hamadans.

Joshagan

This motif derives its name from the central Persian village where it was developed. It is a more delicate variation on the Mina-Khani composition.

Harshang

This word comes from the Persian term for "crab," and represents a crab-shaped flower as well as the shellfish. It was tradi-

tionally associated with Persia and the southern Caucasus, but is now woven into designs from many regions.

Vase

Many styles of rugs employ a vase, or group of vases as the principal design element. Some experts believe the motif was introduced to Persian, Turkish, and Indian weaving from China, where the vase had been used for hundreds of years to symbolize peace and tranquillity. The Zel-i-Sultan design is an allover arrangement of repeating vases of roses, and is considered by some experts to be the most accomplished of all Persian designs.

Gul

Once unique to the Turkoman tribe that wove it, this small rectilinear motif has many variations. A gul motif is often repeated throughout a rug's field and is usually offset with rows of smaller guls. The word "gul" means "flower" in Persian, but the motif's name may have been derived from the ancient Turkish word for family, clan, or tribe. Among Turkoman nomads, the gul motif was used as a tribal emblem, and each tribe had its own distinctive variation. It is also possible that the guls possessed some mystical significance, such as the warding off of the "evil eye." Flemish artist Hans Memling, who used rugs with this motif in many of his paintings, was responsible for the design's renown and influence in Europe. Rugs with the gul design are most closely associated with the town of Bukhara, and are known as Bukhara rugs.

Left, top: The Joshagan carpet from western Iran bears a typical arrangement of diamond-shaped Gul-i-Henna and Mina-Khani patterns.

....

Left, bottom: The Harshang rug reflects a crablike Persian design that is used as a central motif or a repeat pattern.

....

Opposite: This elegant Persian rug exhibits a glorious example of classic guls, in this case the Gul-i-Franc, a French cabbage-rose design.

....

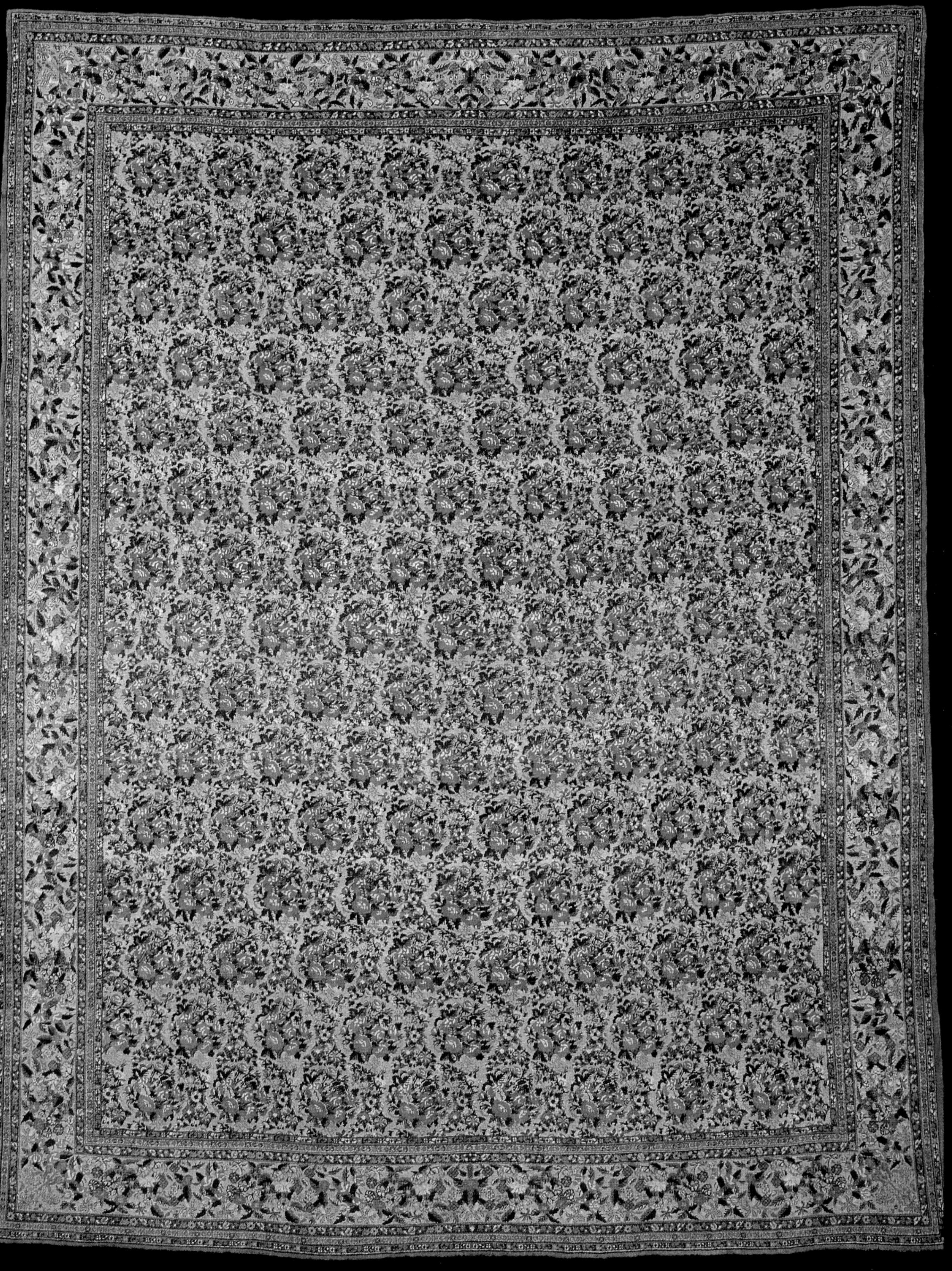

Borders

Oriental rug borders consist of a series of bands, the primary purpose of which is to frame the field of the rug. The standard border ranges from 3 to 7 inches (7.6 to 17.8cm) in width, depending upon the size of the rug, and the overall border may be made up of several smaller borders or simple stripes. Some rugs, such as French Aubusson rugs, have a distinctive design to their border. Other rugs, such as certain Chinese carpets, have no borders at all.

Border motifs vary, and are designed to complement the motifs used in the field. They can be rectilinear or curvilin-ear, reflecting the central motif, and can include flowers, vines, serrated leaves, vases, wine glasses, guls, medallions, and variations on all classic motifs. The variations on these designs are endless.

Inscriptions

Oriental rugs are occasionally woven with an inscription, which can be quite obvious when woven into the background or in a cartouche; others blend more subtly into the central design or border. Inscriptions are usually in Persian or Armenian script, although they can be in Hebrew, Sanskrit, Arabic, or Cyrillic. Persian inscriptions are read from right to left, although numbers are read from left to right. The inscription can be a poem, proverb, prayer, dedication, or simply the signature of the weaver.

Dates also appear on some rugs. Islamic dates, found on Persian or Caucasian rugs, are written in Arabic numerals. These dates are based on the Muslim calendar, which begins with the Prophet Muhammad's flight from Mecca on July 16, A.D. 622. (The Muslim calendar differs from the Gregorian calendar used in the West in that the former is guided by the lunar year.) Western numerals and dates can also be found in some rugs from the Caucasus and Turkey, especially those woven by Armenians. These numerals, when properly interpreted, can be useful for dating antique and semi-antique rugs.

Below, left: Most Oriental rugs have distinctive borders. Persian and Turkish rugs have multibanded borders. Chinese rugs can have elaborate, symbolic borders, like this one, or no border at all.

Opposite: This unusual pictorial Persian rug from Nain bears a large, important inscription that was woven into the sky in the background.

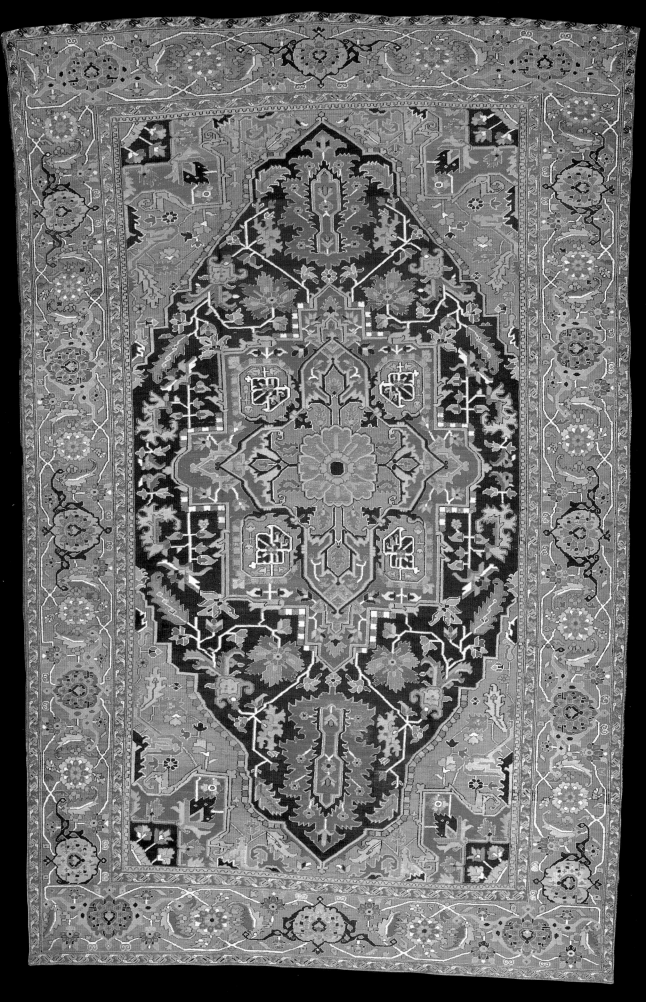

THE WORLD
OF ORIENTAL RUGS

*O*pposite: Karaja rugs are woven in the town of Karaja and the surrounding villages about 35 miles (56km) northeast of Tabriz. They are known by their geometric medallions, their rectilinear floral designs, and their use of madder red and navy blue backgrounds. The blue central flower (above) is exceptionally fine.

As noted earlier, most rugs and carpets commonly referred to as "Oriental rugs" were and are made in the region known as the rug belt, which stretches from Morocco in northwestern Africa to central Asia. However, Oriental rugs have also been produced using traditional Oriental designs and techniques in Eastern Europe, England, France, Spain, and India. In most countries and cultures, some sort of rug design tradition has developed using knotted wool on a flatweave ground. In China, Scandinavia, and the Americas, beautiful wool rugs have been made for centuries using similar weaving techniques, although the final products look nothing like classic Persian rugs.

In today's rug market, however, all these rugs have value—and are often sold as "Oriental" rugs. The following is a brief description of the most active rug-producing countries of the world.

P e r s i a n

R u g s

Persian rugs are those that we most commonly think of when we think of Oriental rugs. These rugs are from what is today known as Iran, although they are still known as "Persian" because this territory was once called Persia. It is bordered by the Alburz Mountains on the north and the Zagros Mountains on the south and west.

The majority of the Iranian peoples are Shiite Muslims, and much of Persian rug design reflects aspects of Muslim culture. Many smaller cultures also pepper the population, including Armenians, Azerbaijanis, Balouchis, Kurds, Bakhtiaris, Turkomans, Qashqa'is, Afshars, Lurs, and Christians. Many of these ethnic groups also weave Persian rugs that reflect their particular culture.

Like most Oriental rugs, those from this region are frequently named for the village where they were made, the group that wove them, or for the town where they were sold. A wide variety of designs, color

combinations, and styles are evident. For most people, memorizing these designs is of no practical use. However, it is helpful to become acquainted with the major Persian centers and the most important Persian rugs, especially those most readily available and of the most assured investment quality. The most significant are: Kashan, Qum, Kerman, Isfahan, Nain, Tabriz, Sarouk, and Hamadan.

K a s h a n   R u g s

Kashan, a large town in central Iran, has produced some of Persia's best classical rugs. In fact, the reputation of the rugs has rubbed off on the town's inhabitants, so that a man who claims to be from Kashan is considered to be a man of quality and style.

Kashan rugs are usually woven with excellent-quality wool pile on a cotton or silk warp and weft, and they tend to range between 200 and 400 knots per square inch. (Kashan also produces some pure silk rugs with 600 knots per square inch.) Colors such as cherry red, yellow, burnt orange, and dark blue are often used to create elaborate diamond-shaped medallion designs. The rugs are very detailed, with many smaller elements such as flowers and birds, and framed with an equally ornate border. One style, known as a "white Kashan" or "five-color Kashan," has been produced since the 1920s primarily for export to the European and American markets, which often prefer rugs made in more delicate colors. White Kashans usually have an ivory or pale blue background with designs woven in various shades of blue and gray.

Left: This map of present-day Iran shows Persia in context with its surrounding countries. It also shows several of today's best-known rug-producing cities.

....

Opposite: This Kashan carpet is a classic example of the elegant rugs that come from the large town of Kashan in central Iran. The intricate central diamond-shaped medallion, jewel-like colors, and the intricate border are typical of rugs from this region. Even modern Kashans, produced for export since the 1920s, are considered excellent investments.

....

Qum Carpets

Qum, also located in central Iran, is best known for its silk rugs, which can be the best in Persian silk rug weaving. Qum also produces some high-quality wool rugs. However, the quality of the rugs in both silk and wool can be uneven. When the rugs are well made, they are excellent; when they are mediocre, they tend to lack distinction of any kind.

Virtually every Qum carpet employs the color turquoise, either in small touches or for the entire background. This color echoes the unique color of the Qum rooftops and does not appear in any other rug from any other area. The designs usually include classic Persian motifs, and are often curvilinear, depicting flowers, birds, and small animals. Since Qum is considered a holy city, the prayer-arch pattern is often used. Almost all Qum rugs have one fringe that is shorter than the other. In fact, one end is often just woven kilim, that is, it has no fringe at all.

Kerman Rugs

Kerman, located in southern Iran, produces some of the most refined and elegant rugs made today. They are usually made of good-quality wool on a cotton foundation with between 200 and 400 knots per square inch. Kerman produces two typical styles of rugs. The first is traditional, displaying classic designs such as medallions, vases, gardens, and allover tree-of-life designs. The second is a soft, curvy central medallion, with smaller, scrolling medallions repeated in the four corners of the carpet, an extremely elaborate border, and an "open" field in just one solid color. Rugs bearing the latter design are sometimes called "American Kermans" because they were developed for the American market in the late nineteenth century. Antique Kerman rugs are considered very valuable, but contemporary rugs can vary in quality.

Isfahan Rugs

Once the capital of Persia, the ancient city of Isfahan in central Iran produces what most experts consider the finest wool-pile rugs in the world. They are certainly among the best modern rugs produced in Iran.

The highest-quality modern Isfahans are made from kurk and are woven on a silk (or combination of silk and cotton) warp and weft at 300 to 400 knots per square inch. In the late nineteenth and early twentieth centuries, Isfahans were all woven on cotton in dark colors and more varied designs. Because they were made under the Qajar dynasty, these rugs are sometimes referred to as Qajar-style Isfahan rugs.

Modern Isfahan rugs are more finely woven than the earlier rugs, but are usually made using pastel colors and finely executed traditional designs that include detailed circular medallions embellished with flowers and entwined tendrils, curving arabesques, and occasionally a bird. The colors and styles are meant to appeal to the European and American markets, and, although modern, they are extremely beautiful. A good-quality Isfahan, whether antique or modern, is considered an absolutely assured investment.

Nain

The tiny central Iranian village of Nain produces incredibly fine rugs, usually woven with 350 to 450 knots per square inch. The best Nain rugs are considered equal to the best Isfahans, with the primary difference being that Nain rugs are woven on a cotton foundation, whereas the best Isfahan rugs are woven on silk or a combination of silk and cotton.

The designs of Nain rugs consist of representations of flowers, birds, and butterflies populating the background, rather than abstract scrolls and botehs. Typical colors in Nain rugs are sapphire blue, ivory, beige, and pale yellow.

In terms of value, superior Nain rugs are usually considered comparable to Isfahan rugs. However, because Isfahan carpets are consistently of top quality, they are probably a more secure investment.

Tabriz

Tabriz, located in the Azerbaijan district of northwestern Iran, was a major center for art trade in the Middle East in the fifteenth century, as it was the nearest Persian city to Europe. Since rugs from throughout Persia would pass through Tabriz on their way to Europe, the weavers there were exposed

*L*eft: Nain rugs are considered to be similar to Isfahans in quality and structure. However, the use of elaborate bird and flower motifs separate Nain rugs and make them very special.

....

*O*pposite: Tabriz rugs tend to vary in quality, but many, like this rug, are incredibly fine. Because the town of Tabriz is a metropolitan center, the styles there also vary. Sometimes the rugs are vivid; other rugs, like this one, are woven in subtle monotones with open backgrounds.

....

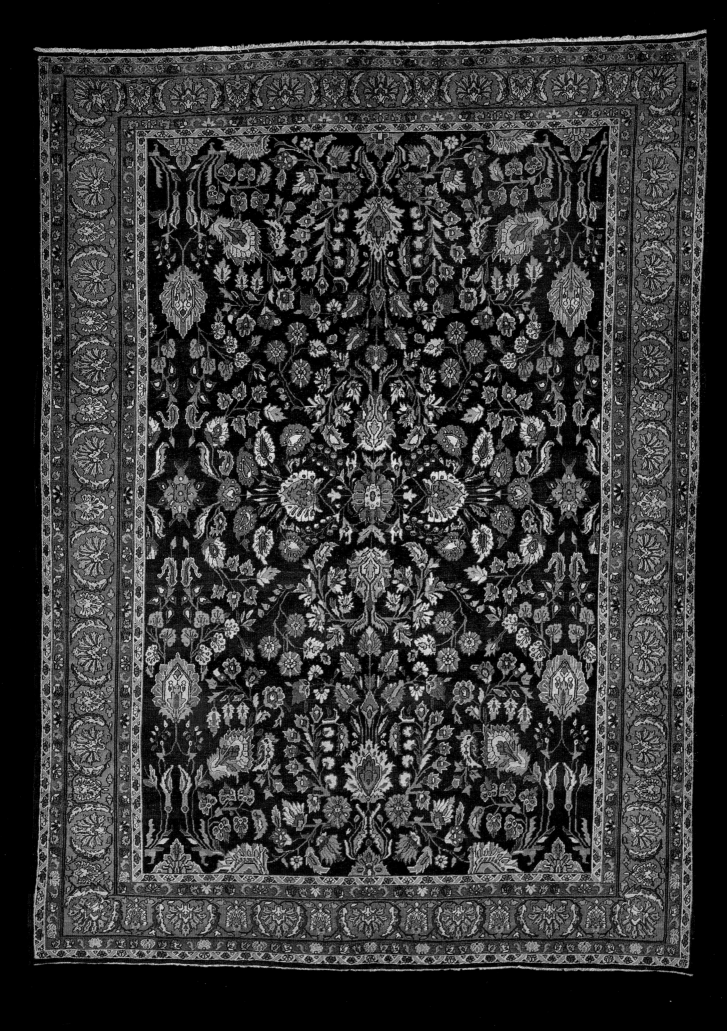

Opposite: Sarouks from central Persia are well known in the United States. They tend to come in two styles: the allover pattern and the central medallion style. Many Sarouks were washed to mute their colors in order to please American tastes.

....

Right: Hamadan rugs come from scores of villages in western Iran. The quality of these rugs vary, and they often cannot compete in intricacy and elegance with the rugs of Isfahan or Nain. However, even the coarser rugs have great charm, especially those bearing a camel-colored background.

....

to the designs of numerous towns, and they copied them freely. Designs imported from China were incorporated into Persian patterns by these weavers. In addition, Tabriz has its own unique pattern, called Taba-Tabriz, which consists of a stylized curvilinear medallion on a cream-colored background with gold-colored flowery borders. The colors of Tabriz rugs vary from soft pastels to darker reds and blues; in general, though, the colors tend to appear in rather muted tones, such as rust instead of red and forest green instead of emerald.

At their best, Tabriz rugs are as finely woven and as aesthetically satisfying as the most accomplished Isfahan or Kashan rugs, but at their worst they can be coarsely knotted and clumsily composed. They are usually knotted with wool pile on cotton foundations, and can vary from 80 to 400 knots per square inch. The local wool is strong but can feel coarse. Tabachi (wool taken from dead sheep) is sometimes used, which results in poor-quality, coarsely textured rugs. A fine-quality Tabriz is a sound investment, but because of variable quality, buyers should exercise care when buying one.

Sarouk

Sarouk, a village in the Arak province of central Iran, lends its name to rugs made in the surrounding area, and most of these are of excellent quality. They are woven with wool pile on a cotton warp and weft, and range between 150 and 400 knots per square inch. Normally, wool of extremely high quality is employed, and

the colors used are rich reds, blues, burnt orange, ocher, and occasionally pale blue, turquoise, or lemon yellow.

Sarouk designs are of two styles: traditional or American. Traditional designs include boteh and Herati composition, in either allover patterns or medallion designs. The American design, also called the Lilihan, features floral sprays radiating outward from a central medallion-shaped floral form. It is so named because it was adapted for the American market from a design originating in the village of Lilihan.

Hamadan

The city of Hamadan, located in west central Iran, lends its name to the rugs made in dozens of small villages whose arti-

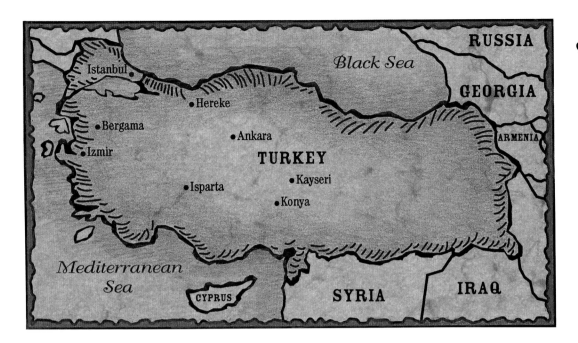

This map of present-day Turkey highlights the important Anatolian rug centers, including Hereke, Konya, Kayseri, Isparta, and Bergama.

sans come to trade in the larger city. Because of the variety of sources, Hamadan rugs can be among the shoddiest and most unattractive rugs made in Iran. However, they can also be well made and exciting rugs, even if they are sometimes rather primitive. Each village or group of villages has its own styles, but some aspects unify them. On the whole, Hamadan rugs tend to be red, blue, or white with touches of green, gold, or ocher. The designs tend to be geometric, with medallions or overall Sarouk or flowery schemes.

All Hamadan rugs are woven on a cotton foundation, with 30 to 100 Turkish (as opposed to Persian) knots per square inch. Usually the wool is of good quality and often it is mixed with camel hair and clipped relatively long. Although Hamadans do not have the investment assurance of some of the finer-quality rugs, they are nonetheless appealing and highly collectible.

Turkish Carpets

It is common in the rug business to refer to Turkish rugs as "Anatolian" carpets. Present-day Turkey (which includes what was formerly known as Anatolia) lies east of the Aegean Sea, south of the Black Sea, and west of Iran. In many ways, Turkey represents a cultural link between the Middle East and Europe.

The art of weaving in the Turkish region is extremely old, perhaps extending back to 3000 B.C. Modern weaving techniques, including the use of the characteristic Turkish, or Ghiordes, knot, can be traced to the Seljuks, a nomadic people from central Asia that conquered the country in the thirteenth century. However, the Seljuks were soon overtaken by the Ottomans from central Asia, whose empire stretched from Vienna to Baghdad and from Crimea to

Libya. The Ottoman Empire reached its peak in the sixteenth century, and its influence is still visible today.

Although the rugs are all called "Turkish," they represent a complex ethnic mixture of Anatolian cultures. Although ethnic Turks form the majority of people living in Turkey, Kurds, who reside in eastern Turkey, constitute a large ethnic minority. The Armenians, Greeks, and Jews who populated Turkey until the 1920s were responsible for weaving large numbers of rugs in Kayseri, Kirshir, Kars, and other towns. Except for Kurdish rugs, which are usually named for their tribe, most Turkish rugs are named for the village or town in which they are woven or sold. In fact, the rugs embody techniques and designs linked to their particular villages. For instance, Kula and Gordes rugs are known for fussy, detailed designs and subdued colors, while Milas rugs are famous for brilliant warm colors, soft wool, red wefts, and flowery designs. Collectors are primarily interested

in a series of Anatolian rug groups called the "traditional provenance groups." These rugs tend to be small and are often prayer rugs.

Turkish rugs first appeared in the West in the late Middle Ages and were probably introduced by Italian traders. Rugs from Turkey were among the first to reach Europe and were known as "Turkey carpets." Thus, for some years, all "Oriental" rugs, including Persian rugs, were known as Turkish rugs. They were first depicted in European paintings in the early fourteenth century in the works of the Seines and Florentine schools, and later in the works of Flemish painters such as Hans Holbein.

Turkish rugs are usually made of wool, silk, or mercerized cotton on a cotton warp and weft. The designs can be either sophisticated and elaborate (curvilinear) or more primitive and geometric (rectilinear). They are usually abstract rather than representational because it is against the Muslim religion to depict any living creature in a

lifelike way. The rugs made in larger towns tend to be light in color with greater use of pastels, probably to appeal to the European market, while the rugs made in smaller villages tend to use darker colors, more popular with Middle Eastern peoples.

The most common design element in Turkish rugs is the prayer arch. A rug that employs a saph design, which consists of multiple mihrabs (prayer arches), has been created for a family, with a mihrab for each family member. In Turkish prayer rugs, a representation of an oil lamp will usually be designed in the middle of the mihrab. In the simpler village rugs, the lamp design is plain; in the sophisticated town rugs, it is a chandelier.

Flowers are often used in designs to represent the garden of paradise. The tulip appears frequently, particularly in antique rugs. (Although Holland is most commonly associated with tulips, tulips are native to the Middle East and were not taken to northern Europe until the sixteenth century.) Occasionally, Arabic script will be woven into the border.

Overall, Turkish rugs tend to be less sophisticated than Persian rugs. The one notable exception is rugs woven in the town of Hereke, which constitute some of the most exquisite rugs in the world. When a Turkish rug is good, it is very good, but those that are inferior can be truly hideous in terms of design, technique, and the quality of the materials. As in Iran, there are scores scores of towns that create indigenous rugs. For the beginner, it is helpful to become familiar with a few of the best known—the ones that create quality rugs as well as the ones that create alluring fakes.

Hereke Rugs

Known as Anacircum by the Romans, Hereke is located at the eastern end of the Sea of Murmur, 40 miles (64.4km) east of Istanbul. In 1843, an imperial factory was founded in Hereke to weave superior rugs for the Ottoman court, and Hereke is still renowned for making the finest silk carpets in the world. The skill, artistry, and technical virtuosity of the Hereke silk weavers is second to none.

Hereke silk-pile rugs are normally woven on silk foundations, although cotton is sometimes used. They are very finely knotted, with about 700 to 800 Turkish knots per square inch. Occasionally, gold and silver metallic threads are woven into the pile. Various shades of red, blue, yellow, gold, and green are the common colors, and these are enhanced by the sheen of the fine silk threads.

Hereke carpets display a variety of designs, many of which have been adapted from Persian carpets. With vines and tendrils filling the field, which often has a central medallion, the patterns tend to be more curvilinear and floral than those emanating from other Turkish weaving centers. The most characteristic Hereke design is that of a prayer rug with a large medallion.

Hereke also produces fine-quality wool rugs. Wool-pile carpets are woven primarily in large sizes; silk in small sizes. Whether wool or silk, Hereke weavers produce very few carpets each year. (The name "Hereke" is also given to many local weavers in surrounding towns, but their rugs are generally inferior.) A true Hereke rug is a treasure, particularly a silk Hereke. However, there are many imitators, and buyers should beware.

Konya

The village of Konya in south central Turkey once made the rugs that Marco Polo described as being the most beautiful in the world. Konya now produces only coarse, primitive rugs, although it is well known for its kilims. In fact, at one time all kilims were called Karamani, named after the province in which Konya is situated. In terms of rug making, Konya is interesting today only for its historic value.

Kayseri

Kayseri is the name used to describe rugs made in a number of villages around the towns of Kayseri and Sivas, which are located in central Turkey. The weavers from this area are known for the variety and inventiveness of their designs, as well as for the quality of their materials and high standard of craftsmanship.

Kayseri is famous for making "art silk" rugs, which are sometimes regarded as being second in quality to Hereke rugs. A few of the carpets are quite beautiful, and unscrupulous dealers may even try to pass them off as Herekes. However, the quality of the rugs is variable, and many are made with mercerized cotton. Called "bazaar pieces," these can fool the naive buyer who has not learned to distinguish silk from cotton. Buyers should be wary and buy only the finest examples.

Spartas

The ancient city of Sparta in southwest Turkey is now called Isparta, and all the rugs of this region are known as "Spartas," although many are made in outlying villages. The weavers of Isparta use the Persian Senneh knot rather than the Turkish Ghiordes knot, and are known for their picture rugs, which are weavings of painting or portraits. In general, the rugs are woven on cotton warps in pastels or earth tones. Many rugs, particularly those woven in town for the tourist trade, are of inferior quality.

Dobag Rugs

The influence of Anatolian rugs declined rapidly after World War I when Ataturk purged the country of Armenians and Greeks, who had been responsible for creating some of the most beautiful rugs. During the revolution, standards of rug design went into a decline, which was exacerbated by the introduction of poor-quality dyes in the 1920s.

In the late 1970s, the government introduced a scheme to improve the quality and profitability of the Turkish rug-making industry. This scheme involved using natural dyes and traditional weaving methods. The result was the creation of the DOBAG, which is an acronym representing the quality restrictions applied by the government on the rug-making trade.

All Dobags are woven with fine-quality wool, dyed with natural dyes, and reflect techniques of a certain level of expertise. The rugs represent a wide variety of traditional Turkish designs, and their color schemes range from rich primary colors to delicate pastels.

Dobag rugs are not called "Dobags" in the marketplace; in the traditional manner, they are named after the town where they were created. You must ask the dealer if the rug is a Dobag. Since this is a recent innovation, the value of Dobag rugs has not been established, but they are usually attractive, durable, and finely made.

Yuruk

The Yuruk are the only nomadic weavers in Turkey. They use a vibrant color palette that includes violet and yellow in addition to reds, blues, and greens as the dominant colors. Yuruks are not particularly finely knotted, but the wool is of good quality and the structure is good. The people weave designs that tend to manifest a Caucasian influence, and they also produce some picture rugs.

Caucasian Rugs

Caucasian rugs were (and are) produced in a region encompassing about 160,000 square miles (414,400 sq km), stretching from the Black Sea in the west to the Caspian Sea in the East, in the most southwesterly part of the Russian empire. For almost a thousand years, this region has been a center of ethnic, cultural, and religious strife, with an unending procession of conquests by Arabs, Persians, Russians, Mongols, and Turks. The indigenous population is equally varied, and includes Christian Armenians and Islamic tribesmen.

This turbulent history is reflected in the bold designs and bright colors used in the rugs of the region. The influence of tradi-

*R*ight: This map illustrates the geographic region where Caucasian rugs are woven. The names of these countries have changed over the centuries, most recently with the breakup of the U.S.S.R. However, today the Caucasian rug region includes parts of southern Russia, Georgia, and Azerbaijan, as well as isolated sections of Turkey and Iran.

*R*ight, bottom: Because of the constantly changing borders, many Caucasian, Turkoman, and Afghan rugs are sometimes referred to as Russian. This particular rug comes from a region of the Republic of Azerbaijan known as Talish. Talish rugs are generally long and narrow with wide borders and a relatively empty center field.

tional Persian, Turkish, and Turkoman designs is evident, but Caucasian rugs are unique and remarkably varied. They often have some unusual subjects, such as insects, human figures, dogs, flowers, and even chickens, as well as more traditional medallions and flowers. The borders of Caucasian rugs are elaborately decorated, and the colors are bright, with a predominant use of blue, red, and green. The weave varies from region to region, but it is relatively fine, with about 250 knots per square inch. The rugs are generally small, 3 by 5 feet (91 by 152cm), and are often made with a wool warp, making them soft and durable.

Because of the unending political turmoil of the region, the rugs do not necessarily bear the names of the towns (or tribes) where they are woven, the way Persian and Turkish rugs do. Many of the old Caucasian

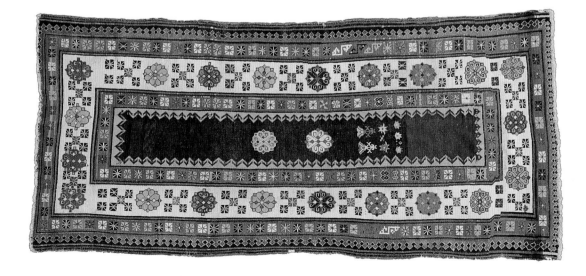

*M*any Caucasian rugs are woven by nomadic tribes, and they are often long and narrow since the nomads work on small, portable looms. This rug is a Karabagh, from the southernmost region of the Caucasus, and features a floral pattern amid a repeat diamond motif. Karabagh rugs are no longer made and tend to be expensive.

....

weaving districts, such as Kazak, Shirvan, Kuba, Baku, and Karabagh, no longer exist under their traditional names or are no longer associated with the rugs bearing their names. For example, a contemporary Shirvan rug may have been made in the Shirvan area, or it could have come from any of the government-controlled weaving centers that produce Caucasian-style rugs.

In contemporary terms, Caucasian rug names reflect the quality or design of the rug rather than its place of origin. The three main grades of contemporary rugs, in descending order of quality, are Shirvan, Kazak, and Derbend. However, any contemporary Caucasian rug may be marketed under the name of the traditional group most closely associated with its design. A prospective buyer must carefully judge each rug on its individual merits, but an attractive and nicely made rug is nearly always a good value for the money.

Turkoman and
Afghan Rugs

The weavers of this region are most famous for the Bukhara design. Although few of the rugs bearing this design are actually made in Bukhara, the major city of the region, they are all traded there. The design consists of an eight-sided gul, about 3 to 5 inches (7.6 to 12.7cm) in diameter, repeated in rows. Representing wisdom, the design looks like an elephant's footprint and is sometimes referred to as such. The footprint is divided by a stylized cross that is meant to resemble a tarantula, which signifies good luck. Some Bukhara designs, called the "Princess" or the "Royal Bukhara," also have a thin line that connects the rows of guls. Despite these regal titles, though, the additional embellishment has no effect upon the value of the rug.

The pattern within the gul varies from rug to rug, depending upon the specific tribe of origin. Moreover, the pattern of an individual tribe can change if a marriage takes place between groups. The three major tribes, all of which are nomadic, are the Tekke, the Salor, and the Yomud. Although the various tribes adorn the inside of the gul in different ways, they mostly use the same materials—wool pile on a cotton base—and color scheme—dark, somber tones—to fashion their rugs.

Baluchi Rugs

Baluchi rugs, which take their name from the nomads who make them, are also woven in the Turkoman region. The major collecting point for Baluchi rugs is the Afghan town of Herat, but the rugs are woven by the wandering peoples throughout the outlying area.

Because they are made by nomads, Baluchi rugs are rarely very large, usually only 3 by 5 feet (91 by 152cm), or if bigger, are merely longer. They are woven on a wool foundation, using rather coarse wool that makes them sometimes a bit irregular. Traditionally, they are woven in dark colors, predominantly blue, red, mauve, and purple. The designs are rectilinear, with abstract guls and stylized flowers, trees, stars, animals, and birds. Another indigenous Turkoman design, the hatchli design, is also frequently used. This design is a large cross that symbolizes the doorposts of a house. Rugs bearing this symbol are often used to mark the doorways of the nomads' tents.

Afghan Rugs

The nomads of Turkmenistan and Afghanistan are closely related in culture, and their rug-weaving techniques and designs reflect this similarity. The Bukhara design is as much a part of Afghanistan's rug culture as it is of the Turkoman culture. The guls of Afghan rugs, however, are much larger than Turkoman guls, and usually measure 7 to 12 inches (17.8 to 30.5cm) across, as opposed to 4 or 5 inches (10.2 or 12.7cm).

Opposite: This Baluchi rug is a particularly fine example of the rugs woven by nomads who roam the vast border between eastern Iran and western Afghanistan. Baluchi rugs are usually woven on wool foundations with a relatively coarse weave. Normally, the rugs feature gul or boteh repeat patterns woven in shades of red and dark blue. Camel coloring is also used, as it is in this rug, and the wool is often an undyed natural color.

The Yomud, or Yomut, is one of the largest Turkoman tribes living in Turkmenistan as well as in northeastern Iran. Normally, Yomud rugs are woven in a repeat gul design of many types or in the cross or hatchli design. The elaborate tree-of-life pattern (opposite) and the vase pattern (right) are relatively unusual for Yomud rugs. Like Baluchi, the Yomud often weave rugs using a pronounced red and blue palette; however, the Yomud are also known for employing lots of white in the borders and backgrounds.

Afghan rugs also tend to be coarser. In general, the wool is variable (sometimes including jute), the dyes are inferior, and the resulting colors are limited—usually muddy reds, blues, and whites.

P a k i s t a n i

R u g s

The country of Pakistan came into existence only after World War II, so it has little history of rug weaving. The weaving industry was organized in 1947, and modern rug-producing methods have been introduced. Indian and Turkoman weavers have emigrated into the area and are producing many good-quality rugs.

Pakistani rugs can be divided into two categories: Bukhara schemes of Turkoman influence, and traditional Persian designs. The former are marketed as Mori Bukharas, and the latter are marketed as Mori Kashans. Regardless of which category they fall under, Pakistani rugs are woven with wool on cotton warps. They are attractive and woven well, but do not have much investment value at this time.

R u g s   o f

I n d i a

India has become one of the largest exporters of Oriental rugs to the West. Producing rugs of all qualities, sizes, and designs, Indian manufacturers have shrewdly analyzed Western tastes and have adapted traditional compositions and designs to produce rugs that will appeal to the Western market.

The rug-making industry of India is based around the towns of Kashmir, Amritsra, Jaipur, Agra, Bhadohi, Mirzapur, Kharmariah, and Ellora. With the exception of those made in Kashmir and Jaipur, the rugs are marketed under the name of the weaving style being copied, not the name of the town. For example, Mirzapur creates rugs imitating French Aubusson designs, so the rugs are called "Aubussons." (Kashmir produces a design

Although Pakistan does not have a long history of rug making and the rugs are not considered to be of high value, there are attractive rugs produced there. This Pakistani rug, woven in wool and silk, is like many rugs produced in Pakistan, in that it was designed in a stylized Persian Malayer pattern.

Right, top: Chinese rugs have a history and style all their own. However, like Persian rugs, the designs and rug quality vary according to the region of origin. Peking rugs like this one are known for their limited color palette of blue, gold, and ivory, and the use of a large central motif like this elegant dragon. The five-clawed dragon, an imperial symbol, is a popular design for rugs woven in Peking.

....

Right, bottom: Dhurrie rugs are some of the best-known examples of Indian rug making. Dhurries are flat-weaves or kilims. Except for very old, rare dhurries, these rugs tend not to have much monetary value.

....

known as the "Vale of Kashmir," based on an elaborate Persian design. These rugs are considered extremely valuable.)

Persian culture has had a profound effect on Indian civilization, particularly with regard to rug weaving. In fact, Indian weavers produce many classic Persian designs. Like Pakistani rugs, Indian rugs are woven with wool on a soft wool warp and weft. The quality of the wools, dyes, and manufacturing techniques improves each year. However, Indian weavers are not encouraged to produce art. Instead, the Indian rugs, though professionally made, are commercial rather than artistic.

Dhurries

Dhurries, famous Indian rugs, are flat-weaves usually woven in simple, geometric designs, making them very inexpensive. Because of their cheapness, they are not normally classified as art rugs, although rare antique dhurries do have some value.

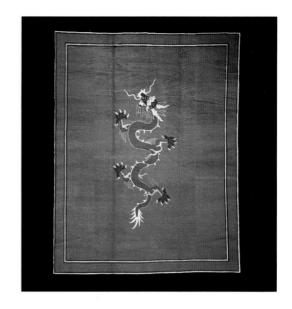

C h i n e s e

R u g s

The origins of Chinese carpet weaving are unclear. It is generally believed that hand-knotted carpets first appeared in China in the third century B.C., and that they were introduced into the region by nomads who had wandered eastward from central Asia. Carpet weaving in China was performed almost exclusively in the northwest region until the late nineteenth century, with the exception of exquisite court carpets woven in Peking (Beijing) during the early 1700s. Early carpets were used as bedding, couch coverings, saddle blankets, and floor coverings. They were also used in Buddhist monasteries as pillar covers, seat and backrest covers, curtains, and prayer mats.

Chinese carpet weaving came under the patronage of the nobility in the late eighteenth century. Nearly a century later, in the 1870s, the Emperor Tu'ung Chich established a school for weaving in

Peking, and a Buddhist monk from Gansu was brought to the workshop to teach. Foreign interest in Chinese carpets arose in the late nineteenth century, and became so great that weaving factories were established in Peking, Tientsin, and other towns, to produce rugs primarily for export. Catering to the foreign market, these manufacturers geared their designs toward Western tastes and demands.

Today, the carpet-weaving industry in China is directed by the Carpet Branch of the China National Native Produce and Animal By-Products Import and Export Corporation, the major branches of which are located in Beijing, Shanghai, Hebei, Shandong, Dalien, Tianjin, and Xinjian. These modern rugs have little investment value, and are, in fact, the only Oriental rugs that actually lose value after they have been used. However, new "reproduction" Chinese rugs that are woven in the antique style using original colors and symbols are worth collecting.

Both antique and modern Chinese carpets are woven exclusively with the asymmetrical, or Persian, knot. The majority are woven on cotton warp and weft threads with wool pile that, on the better rugs, is comparatively deep. (Although thinner piles look similar, they are of inferior quality.) Designs are often embossed by a skilled cutter who carves around the edges of the design to give it a three-dimensional appearance. The rug is then washed to achieve a high gloss.

Silk rugs, which are produced in the province of Shandong—famous for its silk—are woven on a foundation of either cotton or silk warp threads. The most valu-

This Peking rug bears an allover design composed of vases of flowers and other symbols. Unlike Persian rugs, Chinese compositions are simpler and more pictorial.

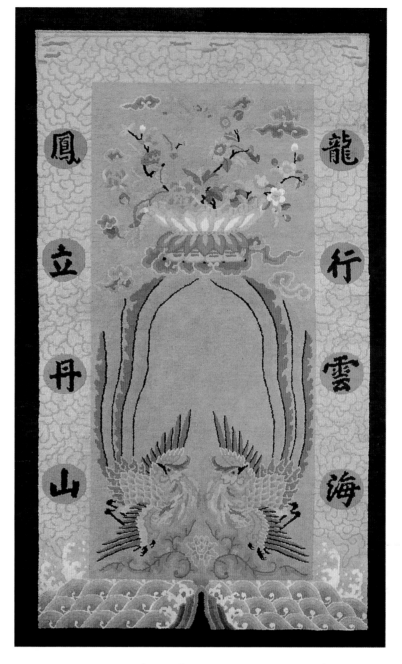

able silk rugs are woven in a traditional style with a high knot count (about 600 knots per square inch), and emulate classic Persian designs. Cheaper, gaudy silk rugs sometimes have gold fringe, even if the warp is made of cotton. Antique rugs were mainly woven in deep and light blue, and cream, as well as beige, rose, and pale green. (Yellow was used too, but only for the emperor.)

The designs woven into Chinese rugs are simpler than those created in the Persian rug-making centers. Most Chinese motifs are crisp and well proportioned. Traditionally, many of the designs are deeply symbolic, inspired by religious beliefs and cultural practices.

Modern Chinese rugs are made in just about every color, including black. Many of the better-known rugs have simple color schemes; for example, the rugs of Gansu are traditionally woven in blue and white. Often, pastels such as pink, pale green, and gold are used.

North African Rugs

Several North African countries, including Egypt, Libya, Morocco, Algeria, and Tunisia, produce rugs. Egypt produces the most important rugs in the region, and has a long and fascinating rug-making history. A number of pile carpets produced in the fifteenth and sixteenth centuries in Egypt are still in existence today, and they manifest a decidedly Persian influence. Modern Egyptian rugs are of quite high quality and are often very expensive, but do not have the investment cachet of a Persian or Turkish rug.

*L*eft, top: This saddlebag comes from Tibet. The border and the flowerlike motifs are distinctly Chinese, but like most Tibetan weaving, this carpet was made for utilitarian purposes.

*L*eft, bottom: This Moroccan rug is woven in a paneled design. Morocco is known for its rug trade, but the rugs are not as high in quality or workmanship as Turkish or Iranian rugs.

Rugs of Tibet and Nepal

Although some traditional rugs are produced in Tibet and Nepal, the rug trade in both countries is minimal. The rugs from Tibet are considered too garish for Western tastes, and they have a decidedly ethnic flavor. Nepal produces some good-quality rugs, which manifest influences of Chinese design and style.

Rugs produced in the remaining North African countries tend to be coarsely made and garish in design. The contemporary rugs are not worth much; however, some antique pieces may be worth collecting.

Romanian Rugs

Folk rug weaving is an old and widespread tradition in southeastern Europe. However, under Ottoman rule, Turkish and Persian influences flourished throughout the Balkans, and most particularly in Romania. Today, weaving in Romania, Bulgaria, and Albania is organized under government supervision with strict standards of quality and appearance. Romania, the largest and most influential of these rug-producing countries, makes

rugs in a broad range of sizes and designs. Each style is named after a town, river, or mountain. However, those names do not necessarily reflect where the rug was made but rather indicate relative quality.

Romanian rugs are woven on either a cotton or wool foundation with a wool pile. The stitches are relatively fine, about 100 to 200 per square inch, and the colors are clear, but not subtle or particularly jewel-like. The designs reflect traditional Turkish and Persian styles. Muslim prayer-rug designs are common, but the rugs often include curvilinear and solid color backgrounds that differ from their Turkish ancestors. Although the rugs tend to be good value for the money (and are a reasonable purchase for home furnishing), most Romanian and Eastern European rugs are not in the "art rug" category, so their resale value is limited.

F r e n c h

R u g s

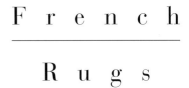

Aubusson and Savonnerie rugs, which are historically products of France, have always been considered "Oriental rugs" even though they are technically European rugs. They are sold with the most valuable Persians, which they equal in craftsmanship.

Rug weaving became popular in France in the early seventeenth century. In 1605, King Henry IV of France, envious of the acclaim the Persian monarchs received because of the quality of their rugs—and because he was unable to secure the fabulous rugs for himself—established a rug-weaving studio in the Louvre. A few years later, the factory was moved to a former

soap factory, which in French is called a savonnerie, and eventually all French pile carpets were known as Savonnerie rugs.

In order to please the king and to decorate his palaces, most Savonneries were created in large sizes. Many were woven with a cream field in colors such as rose, blue, wisteria, and other pastel colors. The field was basically open, but had a few French flower designs. The knotting was relatively coarse compared with that of the excellent Persians, but the wool was thick and of high quality. Many of the rugs were sculpted, creating elaborate three-dimensional designs. The creation of Savonnerie rugs reached its peak during the reign of Louis XIV (1643–1715).

Aubusson rugs are as renowned as Savonnerie rugs. In Flanders, France, and central Europe, a great tapestry tradition had developed in medieval times, and the Gobelins factory, which created exquisite tapestries, was opened in Paris in 1662 under royal patronage. By the time

Left: This Aubusson carpet bears all the classic characteristics of French works of art. These flat-weave tapestries are noted for their soft pastel colors (in this case, rose and ivory), central medallion, elaborate borders, and elegant floral designs.

....

Opposite: This Savonnerie carpet bears the classic characteristics of the Savonnerie atelier, which was originally located in the Louvre and was sponsored by the French kings. While Aubusson rugs are flat-weaves, Savonneries are pile carpets, with knots made with the finest wool in the Turkish knot. Savonneries and Aubussons use similar design elements that are distinctly French.

....

Aubusson, an ancient French tapestry-weaving town, opened carpet workshops in 1743, tapestry making was already an established art form. The Aubusson workshop's objective was to make tapestry rugs in the "Turkish manner," but using French design motifs.

Aubussons are flat-woven or kilim-style rugs; in other words, they have no pile. Like Savonneries, they are usually pastel in color with a cream field and delicate shadings of rose, tan, plum, blue, and other colors mixed in. Often a realistic cluster of roses is positioned in the center, with other flowers in the corners. Curving borders surround the field.

In 1826, a French firm was founded that combined the Savonnerie and Gobelins factories, thus uniting the Savonnerie and Aubusson craft. Neither Savonneries nor Aubussons have been woven in France for generations, and most originals currently reside in museums. Nevertheless, more than passable imitations are produced in India and China.

This Caucasian prayer rug from the late nineteenth century displays a double niche design.

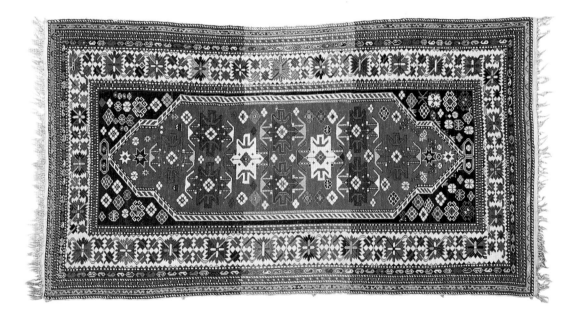

R u s s i a n
R u g s

Caucasian, Turkoman, and Afghan rugs are referred to as "Russian" by some experts, because they come from regions that in relatively recent times fell under Soviet rule. However, since each of these areas has produced unique and powerful designs, Russian rugs, per se, are separated out here.

Russia has been producing rugs since the reign of Catherine the Great (1762–1796). As in other European states with strong monarchies, the early rugs were woven for the royal family with the characteristic eagle design in the corners, a distinctive black background, and a decidedly European feeling to them. These were wool pile knotted on a cotton warp and weft, and the knot count was not terribly fine.

Although rugs are still made in Russia, they are coarse and display somber colors. In these times, Russian rug making is far from thriving.

Greek Rugs

Since pre-Christian times—in fact, since the ancient days of Troy—the Greeks and the Turks have battled over their borders and their peoples. Inevitably, some of their art and culture has shared borders as well. In contemporary rug-making terms, modern Turkish-like rugs have been made in Greece since the 1920s. Greeks who had been living in southern Turkey returned to their native land when Ataturk purged Turkey. Known as Anatolian Greeks, they brought the art of Turkish rug making with them. These rugs are classified as Greek, but they are truly Turkish in craft.

Today, most Greek rugs resemble Persian Kermans, although their knotting is coarser (about 150 knots per square inch). They are made from wool on a cotton warp and weft in government-sponsored workshops. The colors are usually soft pastels in sea green, coral, cream, and turquoise. Floral designs with a simple Persian feel adorn the rugs, which are made of soft wool. However, these attractive rugs tend to be expensive, and do not have the investment value of the true modern Persian or Turkish rugs.

Greeks also make very attractive kilim rugs. The colors are soft pastels in green, blue, and coral. These are also made of coarse wool knotted on a cotton warp and weft. Like Indian dhurries, the rugs are attractive, long-wearing, not expensive, and not of any long-term value.

Spanish Rugs

Spain has an ancient rug-making history. Spanish-Arab rug fragments dating from the twelfth through the fourteenth centuries have been found at Fustat (Old Cairo) in Egypt, and, in the fifteenth century, there were Moorish weavers active in Christian Spain, particularly Alcaraz, Cuenca, and possibly Algeria.

Initially, Turkish patterns were copied from imported Turkish rugs. However, during the fifteenth and seventeenth centuries, wreath motifs with delicate tracery, Christian elements, coats of arms, and other designs were introduced into Spanish designs. The Spanish or "single warp" knot was also developed and used during this time. By the eighteenth century, a purely Spanish form of weaving had developed in the mountainous district of Alpujarras, using an uncut weft-loop pile. Spanish rugs are woven with wool pile on cotton foundations.

Scandinavian Rugs

The Scandinavians have been making rugs since Viking times. The Rya rugs of Sweden and Finland are made using the Turkish knot, but besides this feature, the Scandinavian rug-making sensibility could not be more different from that of the proper rug belt. Their traditional designs are colorful and geometric, with styled floral and figurative elements. The rugs are very loosely woven, with an extremely long "shag" pile.

Scandinavians have also produced many flat-weave rugs. The nineteenth-century double interlocking tapestry bedspreads of the province of Scania, Sweden, have often been mistaken for Balkan kilims, but there is no further indication of a crossing of these cultures.

English Rugs

"Turkey" work coverings, that is, pile rugs from Turkey or those woven in Turkish patterns, were popular in England in the sixteenth and seventeenth centuries. Turkish knots were used in England to create tapestries, but these were usually less tightly woven than "true" Oriental rugs. Nonetheless, good-quality linen and hemp were used for the foundation, and for finer flat-weaves, silk was often used as a weft. However, by the beginning of the eighteenth century, the production of "Turkey work" had come to a virtual standstill. Needlework was preferred for upholstery, and imported Oriental rugs became more readily available for use on the floor.

The art of hand-knotted rug production was revived in England in 1750 when weavers from the Savonnerie factory of Paris opened a shop in London. This particular venture failed, but it gave impetus to Thomas Whitty of Axminster and others to start rug factories. Axminster became famous, and the name was applied to Turkish-knotted rugs produced in England. A type of weave fabricated by modern machines still bears the Axminster name, although the production of the handmade Axminsters declined in the 1820s and finally died.

Handmade rug-weaving was again revived through the efforts of William Morris, who started a rug factory in 1878. Today, rug weaving is confined to craftsmen, and, to some extent, the makers of the famous Donegal carpets of Ireland. Although not finely woven, these carpets are created with good-quality wool in contemporary abstract designs and may have long-term value.

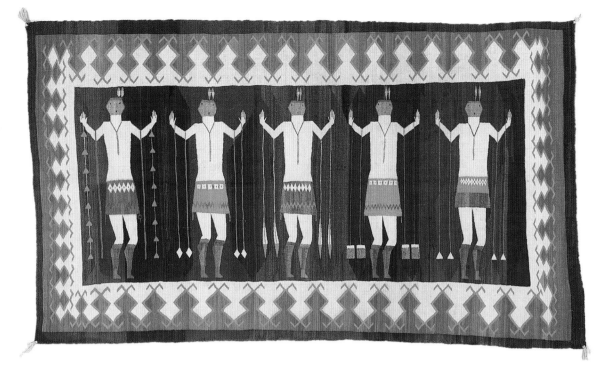

Native American Rugs

Most anthropologists believe that Native American peoples came originally from central Asia, trekked over a narrow spit of land that once linked the North American continent to Asia, and then moved south, settling in scores of locations throughout the North and South American continents. If this is true, it makes them direct descendants of the Mongol peoples, who some experts think began the art of weaving beautiful rugs. It is virtually impossible to prove either point. Nevertheless, certain groups of Native Americans have been weaving remarkable rugs for centuries, and today, those rugs are considered as valuable as many of the most exquisite Persian carpets.

Like their Middle Eastern cousins, no two Navajo rugs are alike. According to Navajo legend, the original inspiration was a goddess called Spider Woman, who taught the women how to weave. (In fact, it has been proven that Navajos learned their craft from the Pueblo Indians in the late seventeenth century.) An important expression of Navajo belief is that one should "walk in beauty," so Navajo tapestries were originally created to be worn. Men wore them draped around their shoulders, and women and children wore blanket dresses. Blankets were also used for bedding, door coverings, saddle blankets, and bags. They were utilitarian and had a reputation for being able to "hold a bucket of water and

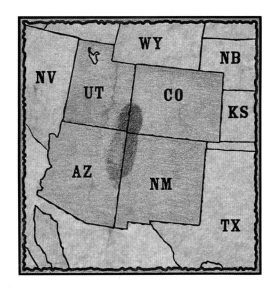

mainly red (cochineal) and blue (indigo)—so sometimes colored yarns were added.

Flannel, dyed with aniline, became available after 1870, and additional colors and machine-spun yarns became available through white settlers after 1875. The result were rugs called "eye dazzlers" because of their bright colors and designs, but the quality of the weaving was not as high.

Between 1890 and 1920, the Indians were convinced that customers would buy floor coverings, so the chief product of the Navajo weaving industry changed to an article best described as a coarse rug. After 1920, the Navajos returned to traditional weaving using traditional materials, so a modern rug may look more like a very old one. The modern revival of Navajo weaving has centered on rugs and wall hangings, and Navajo rugs are made of wool and are woven in bold geometric designs.

Navajo rugs have always been considered valuable. In the 1850s, a cowboy or local settler might pay $50 or $60 for a rug; today, a rug from that period can sell for $50,000 or more.

*L*eft, top: The Navajo rug-weaving region (shaded area). Eleven "centers," each weaving in a different style, are peppered throughout the region.

*L*eft, bottom: This Navajo serape was woven during the so-called Traditional period, 1880–1890.

not lose a drop." At the 1933 World's Fair in Chicago, a fine Navajo rug carpeted the entrance to the New Mexico State exhibit hall. More than 3 million people trekked over it, but by the end of the fair not a thread was broken.

The blankets sought by collectors fall into four stylistic periods: before 1870; 1870 to 1890; 1890 to 1920; and after 1920. Those made before 1870, the most valuable, were woven mainly from hand-spun wool in undyed natural colors such as white, gray, brown, and black. Some natural dyes or colored yarns were available—

This "Eye Dazzler" (top, right), probably from the 1890s, got its name because of the intense effects created by the vivid color combinations. Here, a Navajo woman (top, left) wears a typical rug, and her baby is also wrapped in a warm blanket. This Navajo weaver (bottom, left) sits working at a hand loom that is startlingly similar to those used by Middle Eastern women halfway around the world. This child's serape (bottom, right) was made in 1860 during the Classic period and is woven in the most traditional color, Bayeta red.

Shopping for

Oriental Rugs

Opposite: Buying Oriental rugs is virtually the same throughout the world. Whether you are at an auction in Marrakesh (top), a village road in India (bottom, left), or a village market in Saudi Arabia (bottom, right), a basic knowledge of quality is imperative. *Above:* A detail from an antique Persian rug featuring a relatively open field of design.

A few years ago, I took a trip to Turkey. I had not intended to shop for rugs there at all, but I took a tour, and the guides were as intent upon selling their wares as they were upon showing off their breathtaking ruins.

While in a bazaar in Kasudasi, I had an amusing—and revealing—experience. A little boy kept bringing me rugs he thought were pretty—or perhaps that he suspected I would find pretty. Then he said, in English, "Is your name Pamela?" I could not believe it. How could a ten-year-old Turkish boy come up with an Anglo-Saxon name like mine? Immediately suspicious, I was convinced he had stolen my passport and was not going to give it back to me until I bought a rug. "How did you know that?" I blurted out. "I didn't," he answered, "but I knew you were American and I watch *Dallas* on television every week and Pamela is the only American name I know."

That trip to Turkey, which I took alone, was a great learning experience for me. It was disconcerting to discover that a ten-year-old boy was more sophisticated than I. After all, I couldn't speak a word of Turkish, let alone converse about popular culture in a foreign language. Moreover, this young boy, along with his fellow vendors, knew a lot

more about rugs than I and was also probably aware of the mind-set and rug knowledge of tourists.

My knee-jerk reaction to distrust the young boy stemmed from a general distrust of "rug merchants." In general, rug merchants have a reputation for dishonest pricing and a less-than-straightforward representation of merchandise. Like used-car salesmen, they have a negative stereotype; they are in the business of haggling over the price of a high-priced, used item. But unlike automobiles, rugs are (in theory) handmade, one-of-a-kind, works of art. To put it another way, buyers are often—if not always—at an extreme disadvantage in terms of expertise compared with the seller. When buying Oriental rugs, rule number one is the famous Latin expression: *caveat emptor* (let the buyer beware).

On the other hand, the antique Oriental rug business is equally characterized by knowledgeable dealers who recognize that most buyers are intelligent and discriminating. They know very well that to succeed in their business, it pays to be informative and welcoming. As in the automobile business, the buyer will probably return.

Retail
Dealers

The safest source for buying Oriental rugs, particularly for the novice, is the retail dealer, particularly the department store. In most large cities, Oriental rugs are sold in department stores, such as Macy's,

Bloomingdale's, Marshall Field, and Jordan Marsh. For over a hundred years, these sorts of dealers have been providing fine rugs to the upper crust of their respective cities. Since these stores rely on their reputations and stand by their merchandise, they mostly likely will not intentionally mislead you. But you still should be prepared with some background information; because, unlike in the old-time white-glove department stores of past generations, the salespeople of today frequently lack substantial knowledge about their products.

In many large cities, rugs are also sold in smaller retail shops. Some of the more renowned of these retail dealers are the most important sources for many collectors. Some even produce catalogs of their rugs, which not only provide an indication of the quality of the store, but also serve as a good source of general information about rugs and the rug trade. Various dealers also commission articles about particular rugs written by historians and curators to include in their catalogs. International art and antique fairs in major cities and trade fairs, such as the annual exhibitions presented by the Oriental Rug Retailers of America, are also good places to learn about rugs, especially contemporary ones.

Even the finest rug dealers stock and sell as many—if not more—imitations as real Persian rugs. The American public demands the knockoffs, and many homeowners want carpets that will coordinate with their decor, so they special-order a classic design in particular nontraditional colors. Retail dealers oblige with custom-made rugs, charging from $2,000 to $6,000 for a good 8-by-10-foot (2.4 by 3m) copy. Still, a fine Persian, relatively

new at ten to fifteen years old, will retail for not much more than a brand-new copy, and is probably a better investment. In other words, the made-to-order imitations are expensive and "good" rugs. But they are not one-of-a-kind works of art, and therefore do not have the long-term value of an authentic Persian rug.

A u c t i o n

H o u s e s

Auction houses are another excellent resource for rugs. The major international art auction houses, such as Sotheby's and Christie's, sell everything from Chinese porcelain to modern paintings. Their carpet sales are handled by specialist departments and are always accompanied by catalogs. The carpets are available for viewing in advance of the auction, and the public is usually permitted to examine the rugs. Conditions of the sale are specified in the catalogs, and the authenticity and condition of the rugs are described and attested to according to set standards.

Certain common practices, such as the inclusion of a "reserve" price under which the rug will not be sold, are explained at the beginning of the catalog, and estimates of the range in which the final price will fall are printed. After the sale, the house will send on request a price list that specifies which rugs were bought or which failed to make the

reserve price and remained unsold. This price list can prove educational. You'll begin to get an idea of the current relative values and prices of the best-quality rugs. Carpets deemed to have less artistic or economic stature may be included in second-tier sales of the auction houses. The more affordable prices and the informality of the procedure are designed to make less experienced collectors feel more comfortable.

Buying at an auction house of the caliber of Sotheby's or Christie's is tricky. Although you can be sure that the rugs are fine works of art, your competition for these wonderful pieces consists of highly experienced international buyers who can bid high—especially if the dollar is weak. Buying at this sort of auction requires greater, rather than less, expertise on the part of the buyer. Make sure

This Navajo rug is from the 1920s. Auction houses and fine retail shops often carry American Indian rugs, which are considered to be as valuable as Oriental rugs in some cases.

you know what you are doing. If you are a beginner, going to an auction can be exciting, but refrain from bidding until you are more experienced.

Regional Auctions

Another type of auction house is called the regional house, which has come by its rugs regionally rather than nationally or internationally. Such firms may have specialist departments, and sometimes the quality of the merchandise is on par with that of the large houses. If you are interested in exploring what these smaller organizations have to offer, thumb through the pages of some rug and art magazines for their advertisements. Regional auctions can be excellent sources for Oriental carpets, especially in New England, Washington, D.C., Chicago, and San Francisco, where such rugs were once a standard part of traditional furnishings of sophisticated homes. Often, the auction house is selling the contents of an estate.

Some regional auctions, however, can be quite challenging. Scams are not uncommon, especially those organized by "pickers," who are intermediaries between an established dealer and some of the sources of the dealer's stock. The picker goes to rural antique shops, country auctions, and garage sales with the purpose of buying as many rugs as possible without paying too much. Pickers often know one another, form a "cartel" or "coalition," refrain from bidding against one another, and then settle up later. Sometimes, they even work in conjunction with the auctioneer himself. "Loading a sale" is another unsavory practice, whereby the auctioneer agrees to sell the dregs of a local dealer's store at a sale that has been advertised as the belongings of a fine old mansion. The average buyer cannot know

Throughout the world, buyers can find charming rugs and other textiles being sold right on the street, like this one in Morocco. You must know what you are buying, however, so that you are not cheated.

the intrigue involved. The best advice is, as always, do your homework. But in addition: be pessimistic.

"Flying Carpet" Auctions

One type of sale to avoid completely is known as a "flying carpet sale." These sales are advertised in newspapers as "seized" rugs, or carpets that were never picked up or received at a port of entry. Often held in hotel rooms, these sales tend to include every scam in the book. What's more, the merchandise is almost always bad—if it were good, it wouldn't be there—and the prices are usually high, sometimes higher than those of retail department stores or dealers.

Other Sources

The remaining sources for Oriental rugs are almost infinite. Some are obvious: antique shops, used-furniture stores, flea markets, house sales, garage sales, and your grandmother's attic. As with furniture, you may have a better chance of finding a real prize—or at least a bargain—in an out-of-the-way shop than in a chic vacation spot or large city. For the novice, as long as the price is reasonable and you love the rug, you can do well in these sorts of places.

Finally, you can go directly to the country of origin. Many museums sponsor group tours with the purpose of looking for rugs and informing collectors.

However, whether you go to Russia, China, or Turkey, bear in mind that even the ten-year-olds may well know more than you do. Even—or perhaps especially—when shopping in the country of origin, you need to beware of hucksters, fakes, and overpriced, second-rate rugs.

The Buying Process

Everyone who has been buying Oriental rugs for any length of time has an interesting story to tell about it. My friends Dana and Tom are a classic example. They own several beautiful rugs, some of which they inherited, others of which Dana bought when she was single.

When the two moved into a new house, they found that they needed a large rug to "pull their living room together." They went to several dealers around their Connecticut home, but when they finally found the perfect rug, a Sarouk, the asking price was $14,000, quite a bit more than they wanted to spend. However, when they approached another dealer who had a Sarouk of similar size and condition, they learned that such a rug was probably worth about $5,000.

A few months later, the original dealer telephoned Dana and Tom at home. He asked them if they had found a rug. When they said no, he told them the rug they loved was still at his shop and he was hav-

ing a sale. This time around, Dana and Tom were prepared for battle. They agreed that they would pay no more than $6,000. So when the bartering started, they offered $5,000, wisely naming a figure that was substantially less than what they were willing to pay; the dealer laughed and said he would take $8,000. When Dana came back with "$6,000," the dealer refused to budge. Yet as Dana and Tom started to leave, the dealer pulled them back and took the $6,000.

Bartering. Dana and Tom's story is typical. They ended up participating in the basic process of buying from a retail dealer: bartering. If you are buying retail, the bargaining charade can take hours—or, as in the case of Dana and Tom, weeks.

Some people revel in haggling. They view it as a game, love it when they win, hate it when they lose, and understand that the best approach is to find a place where everybody feels they got something. Other people have an unwavering hatred of bartering. They are shy, self-conscious, and frightened. If you dislike this type of "negotiation" and don't want to spend more than you need to, find a good haggler to help you. (Sometimes a decorator can be a good haggler.) Bartering is an inherent part of rug buying, and you are in danger of being taken if you cannot do it well.

However, even if you are not already well-versed in bartering, you can train yourself. If you are in a store and find a rug you want, buy some time. Sometimes dealers will hold a rug for a few days and, in exclusive shops, will even let you take the rug

home for a day or two, hoping you will become attached to it.

If you are permitted to take the rug home with you for a couple of days, do not take it to another shop to ask the dealer there what he would charge for it. In effect, that is asking for a free appraisal. Dealers know one another and may even refuse to do business with you. It is better, instead, to check out other rugs similar to the one you want. Compare not only price but quality, condition, and age.

Specific Buying Tips. When you decide you want to buy a carpet, begin by doing some research. Read books and magazines, and get an idea of the kind of rug you want. Consider these specific questions:

Do You Trust the Dealer? Has the dealer been in business for a long time? Do you know other collectors who have dealt with

If you are investing a great deal of money, it is useful to know something about the dealer. However, if you are buying a smaller rug during a trip to Morocco, you'll have to rely on your knowledge and common sense.

These beautiful rugs are being sold on a side street in Istanbul. Don't hesitate to explore small dealers and outlets— sometimes great treasures and exquisite rugs can be found in out-of-the-way places.

him? Does he have professional credentials, such as a membership in one of the national associations of rug dealers? Was the dealer open about pricing? Did he point out problems with the rug as well as its attractive aspects? Can you exchange the rug if you find it's unsuitable? What are the guarantees?

Is the Price Right? As with any work of art, there is no infallible way to determine the monetary value of a rug. Even experts disagree. However, through doing your homework, you can begin to get a general idea of the prevailing price for the sort of rug in which you are interested. Check the dealer's catalog, and compare preauction estimates with postauction price lists to figure out if the rug is within a reasonable price range.

Is the Rug Right? First of all, you must find the rug really attractive. Color, design, and texture all play a role in its appeal. Moreover, it is important to consider how the rug will look in your home and how it will fit in with your decor.

Condition. One of the biggest factors in the value of a rug is its condition, which is, in part, determined by the rug's age. Although you want a rug that is in good condition, you should not fear signs of use; value, particularly with older Persians, will always be there. Old rugs almost always show wear and repairs, and some buyers, including experts and collecters, actually prefer the worn look. The key is the extent of the wear and the quality of the repairs. Clearly, the

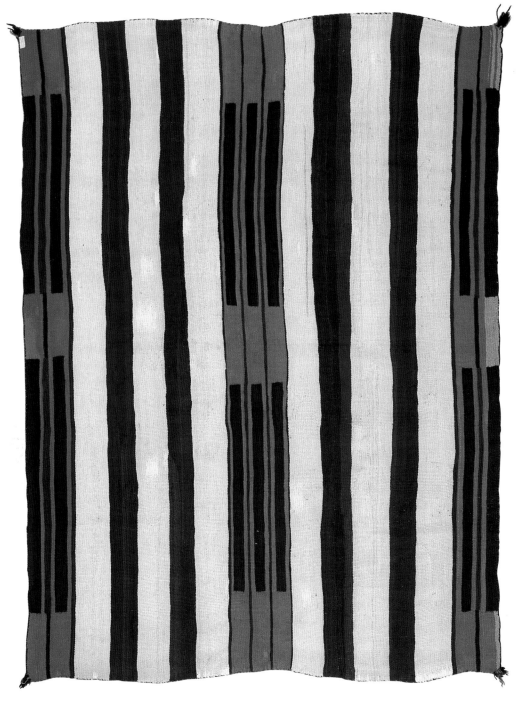

This priceless chief blanket is a beautiful example of Navajo weaving from the Classic period (1850–1875). During this period, the Native Americans acquired yarns from Europe and Germantown, Pennsylvania, and used both native dyes and natural, undyed wools in their rugs.

rug should not be "worn out," but it may have significant value even if highly worn spots are evident. Any repairs should be discreet, and will not affect the value of the rug if they have been done expertly. Even museum masterpieces have repairs!

Remember: finding an old rug in perfect condition is rare. If it looks too good to be true, you are probably not getting as great a deal as you might think.

Integrity of the fabric. Has it been reduced or augmented in size? Shortened or narrowed? Have two rugs been woven together? Have patches been inserted? If the rug has been significantly altered in any of these ways, it may be a beautiful piece, but it is probably not terribly valuable. If you love it, buy it but do not pay a high price for it. Check, too, that the warp and weft are strong. The rug should

*A*lthough most rugs from Afghanistan feature a repeat pattern, usually a gul-like motif, some of the rugs bear stylized figures, flowers, and animals. Also, the color palette normally includes deep reds and blues, whereas this rug has an off-white background. In any case, this unusual rug bears a striking resemblance to Navajo yei designs.

not seem limp or loosely woven. And look for any indications of dry rot by gently folding and pressing the carpet and listening for the "popping" sounds of rotted threads.

Color. Are the colors true, or are they muted? Clear colors indicate that the artisan has used good-quality dyes and techniques, whereas muddy colors indicate the use of poorer dyes and the possibility of chemical painting.

Are the colors faded? Fading can actually be quite beautiful, especially in antique rugs, but the fading should not appear extreme. Check for strident changes in color, which indicate the use of poor-quality dyes. Is the "abrash" harsh, or muted and gentle? Is there evidence that the colors have been chemically altered? Is there evidence of "painting" with felt-tip markers on the warp or weft? Ask to view the carpet in natural light against the nap. The dark colors should jump to life and take on different shades.

Dyeing techniques. Most new carpets are synthetically dyed, but colorfast; antique ones, on the other hand, are vegetable-dyed and may have faded or run. Nonetheless, the latter are priceless. A large group of rugs that are truly antique, but of poor quality may have been chemically treated or "painted" (to give them an aged look) through a process that may not have worked, in which case the dye will come off. Wet the corner a white handkerchief or tissue with saliva and rub it here and there over the carpet. If no color comes up, it is fine.

Pile. Rub your hand along the face of the rug and feel the texture of the pile. Brittle fibers will not last as long as soft ones. Separate the fibers to see if the color on the top matches the color on the bottom. If the color is different, the rug has been painted. Is the pile in good condition? If the pile is worn, is it worn in spots (which is to be expected), or overall (indicating artificial aging)?

Basic Structure. Is the structure appropriate to its design, age, and type? Are the materials appropriate? Are the warps cotton or wool? Familiarize yourself with the difference by examining the fringes of new rugs that use both. Are the materials used appropriate to the type and origins of the rug in question? If not, do they suggest that the rug is a copy or that it has been restored? If the pile is supposed to have silk, is it really silk, which will make the pile soft and delicate, or mercerized cotton, which will have a rougher texture?

Designs. Familiarize yourself with designs, perhaps starting with rugs you admire most, so that you begin to recognize classic examples. For example, many Persian rugs have center medallions and heavy borders. Persian rugs from Tabriz, Sarouk, Kerman, Kashan, Isfahan, and Nain have curvilinear and flowing designs, while Caucasian rugs often feature bold, geometric designs with center medallions. With this type of basic background information, you will be able to converse about rugs with greater ease, confidence, and knowledge.

Do You Know What You Are Doing?

Some experts advise you to act smart even if you don't know a thing. Their feeling is that with some dealers, you may pay dearly for ignorance. Other experts, however, think that it is a good idea to admit to dealers that you are a beginner, the idea being that the dealer may be more informative. For novices, perhaps the best advice is simply to hide your feel-

Opposite: This Sarouk is unusual in that it is woven in a soft camel color as opposed to the traditional ruby red or dark blue. However, the vase designs, flower sprigs, and elegant border are typical of rugs of this type. Also, note that the abrash, or color striation, is subtle and muted, indicating that this is a rug of superb quality.

This remarkable display of kilim rugs at a bazaar in Istanbul is a perfect illustration of the variety of rugs you can find in any shop or market around the world. Remember, if you love the rug and can afford it, chances are you have not made a mistake with your purchase.

ings. While looking at the rugs, demonstrate general enthusiasm, be friendly with the dealer, ask questions, but don't admit that you are utterly ignorant. And on top of everything, when you see the rug of your dreams, do not let the dealer see how much you desperately want it, or you'll end up having to pay an arm and a leg.

Particularly, don't make an offer unless you truly intend to buy, even if you end up not coming to terms. Don't waste the dealer's time by toying with him. Also, have your particular price in mind. On the other hand, don't make a ridiculous offer, which may jeopardize the respect of the dealer for you. Be honest and relatively straight-forward. Remember, the dealer wants your business.

What If You Make a Mistake?

Every buyer goes through a series of "what if?" feelings. What if you buy this rug and tomorrow find something you like better? What if you offer an unacceptable amount? Will you blow the deal? What if you find a cheaper rug next week? What if you missed a defect in the rug or made some other gross error? What if you discover this is a reproduction?

The bottom line is: if you like the piece, if you have asked lots of questions, if you have confidence in the dealer, then don't wait. Buy it. Finding a better rug for more—or for less—often happens, but so what?

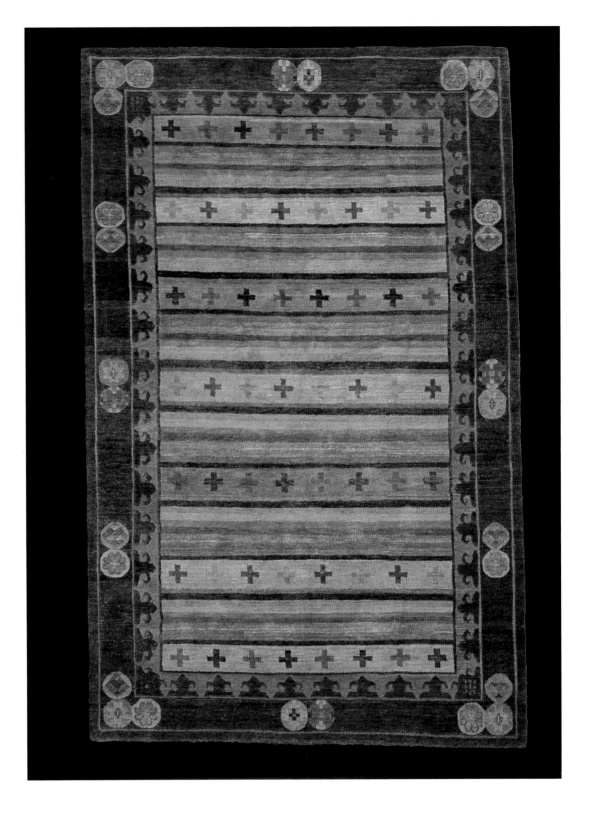

This Amdo-Caravan rug, woven by nomadic weavers, shows a remarkable sophistication of color, design, and style. A rug need not be a masterpiece to have tremendous charm and potential value.

However, what if a month later you realize that you paid too much for a rug? You have a number of recourses. You can try to return it, but if it was an honest sale, this course of action may not be possible. You can hang it on your wall as a constant reminder of the importance of humility. Or you can resell it, suckering someone else for the price you paid or else taking a loss. In any case, this last scenario gets the rug out of your sight.

Occasionally, you may run into a true case of misrepresentation. If you bought the rug at an auction, check the "conditions of sale" section of the auction catalog. With most reputable auction houses, a rug can be returned within a stipulated amount of time for a refund.

In most states, the law defining misrepresentation is not confined merely to making false statements, such as misrepresenting a Kerman as a Kashan, but also applies to errors of omission, such as neglecting to inform you that the rug has serious dry rot. With regard to egregious overcharging, only brand-new rugs have a standard wholesale price per square foot, determined by the type and quality. With antique pieces, overpricing is much more difficult to prove. There is always a difference in price as experts often disagree.

Collecting
and
Investing

New rug buyers must acquire knowledge. If you are embarking upon creating a serious collection, you need to know all about rugs. What's more, you also need to know about the "rug world," the fads, fashions, and the current situation regarding supply and demand.

To start, visit local dealers regularly. Get to know the owner, and discuss the rugs in stock. Examine rugs closely; compare several side by side, and ask questions. Obviously, in a business where haggling is central, there is a strong tradition of secrecy. Some—perhaps most—dealers don't put price tags on the merchandise. Most dealers will discuss price with individuals who seem serious about purchasing rugs. Like anything, certain rugs are "hot" at particular times, and the trendy items will be more expensive. Before you buy, check dealer catalogs, auction catalogs, and rug magazines like *Hali* and *Original Rug Review*.

Investing
Rugs are one of the best investments you can make—almost as good as real estate, and better than antique furniture. With regard to investing in art, it is easier to collect rugs than paintings. Once you know just a bit about the history, you can be fairly certain of getting something of value—and something whose value will rise. In recent years, the demand for rugs and their value has soared.

Because of the volatile political situation in Iran, the price of Persian rugs has varied tremendously over the past twenty years. When the Shah was overthrown in the early 1980s, rug prices fell. In recent years, because of an embargo on Iranian goods, rugs cannot be imported directly from Iran. Today, even importing Persian rugs from other countries is complicated, making the value of good Persians rise. At the same time, other countries, such as Pakistan, India, Romania, China, and Turkey—the other primary producers of carpets—have increased their output, making their rugs more affordable. Finally, the value of the dollar fluctuates constantly, which also affects prices.

Nevertheless, the international trade in Oriental carpets has gone on for centuries, and regardless of the particular politics of the day, it will continue. It makes purchasing trickier, but for long-term investments, rugs remain a good buy.

The Antique Quandary

Oriental rugs fall into three categories: contemporary (twenty-five years old or less); semi-antique (twenty-five to fifty years old); and antique (anything over fifty years old). The antique rugs are the ones most sought after by dealers and collectors, with the greatest interest being in rugs from tribal villages.

The price range for Oriental rugs is vast. A typical dealer will stock rugs ranging from $300 to $100,000. Today, you can expect to pay about $7,000 for an exceptional-quality 9-by-12-foot (2.7 by 3.7m) contemporary Caucasian rug. An authentic antique piece of the same size will cost $20,000 and up, depending on quality and age.

Obviously, the investment value of a rug has to do with beauty, workmanship, durability (good rugs have a floor life of eighty to a hundred years), and quality. Since the end of World War II, rug weaving has become increasingly modernized. Many imported rugs are made in factories, chemical dyes are used, and patterns are mass-produced. As a result, carpets made by hand are becoming a lost art form, especially among the tribal people. Therefore, a rug's value rests not only on its beauty, but also on its uniqueness.

Investing can be very tricky. It requires patience and a great deal of research in order to make an informed choice. In general, Oriental carpets are a medium- to long-term investment. Only an informed expert can make a quick killing; novices should plan to hang on to a rug for at least five years.

This rug is attributed to the Kuba weavers of the northern Caucasus. Kuba rugs often have elaborate, stylized floral designs in the center. Kubas are considered to be among the most valued antiques, but even experts question their provenance.

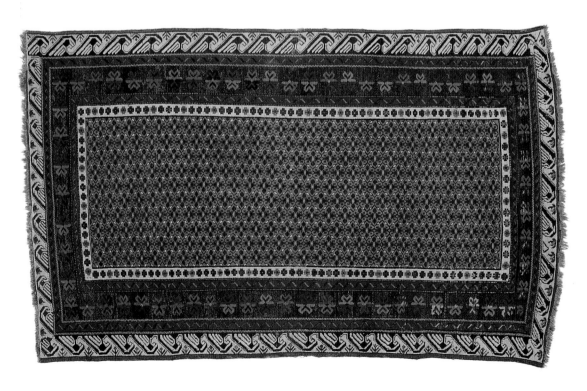

DISPLAYING

ORIENTAL RUGS

Opposite: If you have a particularly exquisite Oriental rug, try to display it to its best advantage. Place it in a space where it can be seen, but that's also big enough to provide space around the edge to "frame" the carpet. Above: Most retail shops sell pillows made from old rugs, but sometimes you can find damaged rugs that can be made up into lovely accessories at flea markets for virtually nothing.

Traditionally, Oriental rugs were created to be used as floor coverings. This was true regardless of where they came from: Iran, Turkey, North Africa, India, or China. In Persia, the classical arrangement involved the placement of a large, exquisite rug at the center of the room with long, thin runners placed along the sides and at the ends. Persians also used rugs to cover pillows, walls, pillars, tables, chairs, and benches. Homemakers hung the rugs on the wall to create a cushion for the backs of people sitting on backless benches against the wall.

When rugs were first brought to Europe, they were available only to the very wealthy. Still, although buyers were thrilled by the jewel-like beauty of their exotic rugs, they continued to use them for functional purposes. Of course, they were used as floor coverings, but they were also employed as cloths for tables and chairs, and, in colder climates, as curtains for windows and doors.

Rugs, no matter how ravishingly beautiful, were always meant to be used. Even serious collectors of very valuable carpets place their rugs on the floor. However, like any beautiful object, it is helpful to place rugs strategically and to light them well.

Decorating:
A Few Thoughts

This is not a book about how to decorate with rugs. However, here are a few ideas to consider when you are looking to buy a rug for use in a particular area of your home.

The Issue of Size

People often end up buying a rug that is too large for the room they are decorating. We often think of a "room-size" rug as "wall-to-wall carpeting," but in fact, a relatively wide border of wood floor should surround the rug in order to balance the rug and to allow the pattern to be more visible.

And a room-sized rug is not the only option for covering the floor of a large room. Using several smaller rugs in such a space adds variety and can actually help to create and delineate smaller areas within the larger space. This decorative ploy also works in average-size rooms, which can be divided using two or more mid-size rugs. I live in a typical New York apartment (a space considered small by most North Americans), but I have the space divided into an entryway, a sitting area, and an office, each with a different rug defining the perimeters.

Because an Oriental rug is rich-looking and warm, the bedroom is an ideal place for it. It can be used as a floor cover, but when placed on a wall or draped across a bed, it can create a luxurious effect.

Hallways can be enhanced dramatically with the use of a long runner. Used in a kitchen, this Oriental rug creates a welcome atmosphere of elegance and warmth.

Color and Style

Many serious collectors view their rugs as works of art and either furnish their home around them or consider their rug collection as something completely separate from the concept of "home furnishing." On the other hand, many people who genuinely love rugs and respect their artistic value look for a particular rug—or rugs—to enhance their decor.

Today, pastel shades have become popular, and the traditional jewel-tone rugs are out of favor. (Most experts turn up their noses at this trend, and cling to the idea that traditional coloring of a fine Oriental has a financial value and practical advantage.) Created with vegetable dyes, the older rugs fade in such a way that a hundred years or more later, the rug looks more beautiful than the day it was completed. Nevertheless, Eastern producers are exporting many beautiful pastel-colored rugs that may well be extremely valuable in years to come. So, if rugs of a particular color scheme suit your taste and your decor, you should buy them.

Style is also a consideration. In general, a pastel-colored, curvilinear Chinese rug will probably not go well with a dark-colored, rectilinear Caucasian rug, but perhaps that depends upon the rugs themselves and the style of the house. Or perhaps you prefer one style in one room, and another style in another.

Creative Uses

From an economic point of view, it is usually wise to buy the best rugs that you can afford, and avoid investing in a particular rug just because it looks like a good deal. It is also fun to keep an eye out for small, terribly worn or dirty pieces that can be used throughout your house.

Dana and Tom, my friends who ultimately got a bargain on a Sarouk, have tiny Oriental rugs in their "mud" room. Other friends throw a worn, but softly interesting Oriental over their sofa so that their dog can rest comfortably. They also have old Orientals placed over the brick floor in their kitchen, giving the room both beauty and warmth. I have a television table that I cover with a Greek kilim, which adds color and charm to an otherwise hideous piece of furniture.

The library (or any other room filled with books) is an ideal place for an Oriental rug. Older, worn rugs are perfect throws for chairs and couches. Any seat that endures lots of wear and tear can use an Oriental.

*O*riental rugs, especially softer flatweaves, can work well as tablecloths or as padding underneath a white lace cloth. In this room, Oriental rugs are used on the floor, on the window seat, as a curtain, and as pillows.

A *F*ew *P*ractical *C*onsiderations

Oriental rugs are meant to be used. However, to preserve the beauty of your rugs, it is important to minimize wear and tear, dirt, and exposure to large amounts of sunlight, heat, or other elements that might damage them.

Special care should be taken with regard to putting rugs in the dining room, which is a popular place for Oriental rugs. Moreover, care should be taken in the choice of the rug. Do not select a rug with a beautiful central medallion design that will be hidden under the table. Also, try to turn the rug at least once a year so that certain areas are not ruined by table legs and chairs being pushed in and out. Finally, of course, clean up any spilled food or drink immediately (see page 118).

Certain rugs—kilims, silk rugs, and worn-but-valuable antiques, particularly—should probably not be used on floors. These rugs are fragile, and should be treated with extra care. If you do use them as a floor covering, place them somewhere that does not get much traffic.

Rugs can be used effectively as coverings on tables, but take similar care. Protect them from food, drink, and candle wax by covering the rug with a linen table cloth. Do not cover a rug with glass or a sheet of plastic because moisture tends to accumulate, which can cause dry rot in the rug and ruin the wood on the table as well. Small rugs can be framed quite beautifully, but make sure moisture does not collect on them. Finally, don't place flower pots or planters directly on a good rug.

Hanging on Walls

Hanging rugs on the wall can be a marvelous way to display rugs, and is perhaps a better way to show off more valuable carpets. Whenever hanging pile rugs, make sure the pile is going down to minimize the accumulation of dirt. Be sure to hang heavy slit-tapestry kilims vertically, since the wefts are not continuous across the rug; hanging them horizontally causes the slits to gape open, thereby weakening the fabric.

Most museums hang rugs by using that marvelous invention: Velcro. First, machine-sew one strip to a piece of heavy, prewashed cotton, and then hand-sew the strip carefully to the back of the rug with linen or cotton carpet thread. Staple the "hook" strip to a beveled strip of wood. Then bolt the wood to the wall and affix the rug in place. If you have a large rug, you may want to put Velcro strips on the sides and bottom to keep corners from curling.

Another method of hanging is to create a sleeve by carefully hand-sewing a strip of heavy cotton to the back of the rug and then inserting a curtain rod. Still another method, which works especially well for smaller rugs, involves attaching metal clips that hang from a curtain rod, rather like a shower curtain. Finally, it is not necessarily bad to simply nail a rug to the wall, but make sure you carefully insert thin nails so that you do not needlessly break threads. Small, thin rugs can also be mounted on cotton or linen canvas stretchers that are available at art supply stores and framed.

Do not hang rugs over hot-air vents, space heaters, coal or wood stoves, humidifiers, or places with extreme temperature or moving streams of air. Place spotlights or heat-producing lamps at a safe distance, and avoid hanging a rug in direct sunlight.

$\mathcal{R}$egardless of the size of the wall—or the rug—Oriental rugs make marvelous wall hangings. This high, dramatic tiled wall is warmed by the presence of a large framed rug. Hanging rugs on walls is also a good solution for more delicate rugs. Lighting should also be considered. A beautiful rug should be carefully lit so that it can be seen to advantage. At the same time, it should not be hung where it would receive direct sunlight, which could cause fading.

CARE AND REPAIR OF

ORIENTAL RUGS

Opposite: One of the most fascinating things about decorating with Oriental rugs is that different styles can be easily combined. Here, a rustic Caucasian rug in an entryway lies near an ornate Persian carpet. The effect is elegant and warm. Above: This detail depicts an exquisite and elaborate sample of a Persian repeat design.

Anyone who loves Oriental rugs believes that they are true works of art. However, in the case of a Monet or a Matisse, you would not think of repairing a chip of paint with a permanent marker or of placing a piece of cellophane tape over a small rip. However, incredibly, one can make just such repairs on certain Oriental rugs without affecting their beauty or their value.

Oriental rugs are tough. These rugs are not like run-of-the mill broadloom carpets, created with tufts of manmade fiber looped loosely around a polyester warp. These are strong weaves, created with thousands of knots of animal wool, hand-knotted onto a tight foundation that is made of wool, cotton, or silk. If they are treated with care and respect, they should last for generations—if they haven't already.

Of course, like everything else, rugs get dirty, worn, and sometimes damaged. Despite their sturdiness, the weight of a dining table, the tracking of feet, or the effects of sunlight can take their toll. Even everyday vacuuming, sweeping, and washing can be hard on them. This chapter will tell you how to care for all your rugs, from your beloved but a bit worn Hamadan to your priceless Shirvan.

Everyday

Maintenance

Providing proper padding is one of the most important aspects of rug care. A pad not only keeps the rug from slipping on a floor, but it protects it from the wear of shoes and furniture, not only on its face, but on its back, or foundation, which is equally important.

Although padding is available in many styles at many prices, it is important to buy the best quality you can. Old-fashioned felt padding is still optimal, but good-quality synthetic rubber is also fine. Do not buy cheap rubber or foam rubber, for these wear out quickly, lack adequate cushioning, and tend to collect moisture, which can damage both the rug and the wood floor underneath.

Many people place smaller Oriental rugs over wall-to-wall broadloom as an accent. With this setup, the bottom layer of carpeting becomes the padding by default. However, use this decorative device only with short-pile wall-to-wall carpeting. Not only is the look of shag carpeting next to an Oriental rather unattractive, but the Oriental overlay will not stay smooth and secure.

Although it is often impossible to avoid placing furniture on top of a rug, especially a large one, wood furniture

By creatively using a lovely Oriental rug, you can turn a fussy bedroom into an elegant bedroom and sitting room, perfect for reading, writing, or dreaming.

is certainly acceptable; metal chair and table legs, or sharp wooden legs, can cut or damage the wool, and should be avoided at all costs.

Move your rugs frequently, as you do your mattress. If indentations form, take out steam iron and set it on "wool." (In the case of a silk rug, use the "silk" setting.) Place a damp towel over the indentation and then steam it for a minute or two.

Keep your rugs away from direct light, especially sunlight, but also from strong artificial light, such as a spotlight.

Although harmonious fading is a part of the rug's fine look—and antique rugs, especially, are certain to fade—it is best that exposure to the sun be minimal.

Vacuuming

Even if you have an antique that was woven before the invention of the vacuum cleaner, do not be afraid to use this twentieth-century device on it. However, make sure to set the vacuum cleaner's brushes on the highest point, sometimes called "shag," so that they are not "beating" on the rug as you vacuum. With silk or very fragile wool rugs, use a carpet sweeper, shake the rug lightly, or brush it by hand using soft nylon bristles.

Moths love wool rugs, so while you are vacuuming, pay special attention to evidence of moth visitation. Vacuum or brush rug corners in dark, hidden places, such as behind a chair or underneath sofas. Backs of wall hangings are also attractive to moths. Moth-proof sprays are available, but the chemicals could damage a valuable rug. Instead of using these artificial substances, put baskets of feathers in a hidden corner; the moths will lay their eggs there.

Any obvious stain on a rug—food, wine, shoe polish, coffee, tea—should be cleaned immediately. There are many books on the subject of spot removal. Quickly blot up the

This Chinese rug bearing an open background with symbolic birds and flowers comes from Yarkand, an area in Eastern Turkistan. Many rugs from this area of China have a strong Persian influence.

This rug boasts a classic Herez design with a large rectilinear medallion, spandrels in the corners, and stylized leaves throughout. In fact, this rug was woven in China and is a fine example of the beautiful rugs produced there in recent decades using classic Persian designs.

mess, keeping the rug flat. Use a gentle soap except on a silk rug, which should be cleaned with vinegar water.

Rugs should be washed about once a year. However, before you begin, you should check that the rug will not bleed when wet. (Put saliva on a white handkerchief, and rub it over the various colors of the rug.) If you think the rug will bleed, have it cleaned professionally.

You can wash small rugs yourself, in the same way you would hand-wash a favorite wool or cashmere sweater. Remember, these rugs are made of natural fibers, just like a good wool sweater. Use a neutral-pH detergent, like Orvus, Woolite, baby shampoo, or pure soap flakes.

It's usually best to wash rugs on a warm, sunny, summer day. Even a small rug will get very heavy once it is wet, so you might want to wash outdoors using a hose. Once the wash is complete, allow the rug to dry by hanging it on a rack in a place where it will receive lots of air. Letting it dry outdoors is best.

Never shampoo a silk rug. Instead, make a vinegar and cool water solution (one part vinegar to three parts water). Spread the rug out flat, and using a clean chamois cloth, gently rub the surface of the rug with the vinegar and water, always stroking in the direction of the pile. Air-dry the rug away from direct heat.

Professional Cleaning

Being made of natural fibers, most rugs require less professional cleaning than you may think, probably only once every five to seven years. In fact, many experts believe that professional cleaning may actually damage the rug.

Even if you are taking your rug to a professional cleaner, it's a good idea to know whether the rug is colorfast. Test the color using the handkerchief test. If the handkerchief is stained from any of the colors, you may have a problem because the rug will run when it is wet.

Especially if your rug fails the handkerchief test, ask your nearest Oriental rug dealer to arrange to have the rug cleaned. Tell him that the colors may not be fast. If the store can't help you, call one of the better-known auction houses like Sotheby's or Christie's, which will recommend specialist rug cleaners, or contact National Institute of Rug Cleaners, 1009 North 14th Street, Arlington, VA 22201, 703-524-8120.

Never take your rug to your local dry cleaner. Cleaning works of art is not the specialty of the neighborhood dry cleaner, even if he proudly says it is. Dry-cleaning chemicals are toxic and may damage the wool, patina, or coloring of your rug.

Everyday Remedies for Repairing Everyday Rugs

The cliché "A stitch in time saves nine" is particularly apt with regard to Oriental rugs. Although you would never dab a quick spot of acrylic paint on a little crack on your Monet, applying small stitches here and there on an Oriental rug is perfectly acceptable.

In fact, it can be useful to do some rather elaborate repair work on old, beloved rugs. (For valuable rugs, get professional help.) For small rugs with weak areas, sew a felt pad over the entire back, which will give it extra padding. Use transparent Scotch tape pressed to the back of the rug to prevent a small hole that you can't fix immediately from getting worse. When you do get around to fixing the hole, darn the worn area the same way you would darn a sock. Weave with small stitches using crewel embroidery thread. Don't cut away loose threads; just fold them back out of sight.

For larger holes, consider making a patch by using a piece from another rug. Ask your dealer for fragments, cut the patch to size, and sew it in position, matching up the lines and colors as best you can.

If the fringe is unraveling, stop it by taking a few defensive stitches using a heavy linen thread and a blanket stitch. For a quick, temporary fix, use transparent Scotch tape. If the fringe is looking rat-

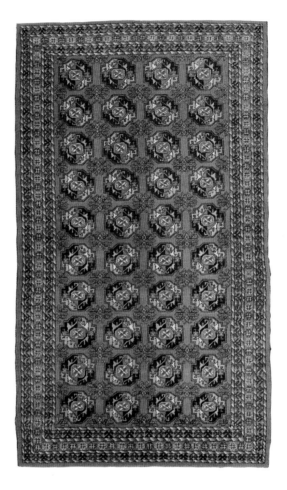

This rug is woven in a classic Bokara repeat pattern with traditional Bokara coloring. In fact, this is a contemporary Chinese rug produced in the Persian style. These rugs are often finely made and can make good long-term investments.

ty, never cut it off. Simply fold it under and lightly stitch it in place; knot it or braid it.

Repairing Good Rugs

These spit-and-polish remedies are not acceptable if you need to repair a very valuable rug. Also, if a good rug has structural damage (damage to the warp and weft), only professional repairing will do. Antique rugs should always be taken to a professional repairer to be rewoven. The repairs are usually very expensive (you

should not be able to find the repair) but it is well worth the money.

Research the repairer's work carefully. To find a reputable repairer, ask your local rug dealer or department store, a museum curator, a rug-cleaning company, or an auctioneer.

Storing

Many collectors store their heavy wool rugs during warm months and bring out their light kilims, which they have stored during the winter. Other people store rugs that they simply have no use for at the moment. In any case, rugs need to be stored with special care, particularly to avoid moisture and moths.

Store small rugs flat, preferably wrapped in acid-free paper in textile storage boxes, which can be purchased from archival and conservation supply firms and are often advertised in catalogs. Larger rugs should be rolled, never folded. Use acid-free cardboard tubes with acid-free paper. Make sure the rugs are clean, especially insect-free, before you put them in storage. It is important to keep them in a place that has been mothproofed.

Insuring

Finally, it is a good idea to insure your rugs, just as you would insure any valuable art collection. Your investment can be wiped out by fire, flood, or skilled thieves. Ask your insurance broker for advice. The insurance probably will not be terribly expensive, and it is well worth any price.

GLOSSARY OF RUG TERMS

Abrash: A color variation or stripe of a slightly different hue across the body of a carpet, the result of a slight color difference in the dye lots used.

Allover Design: A rug field pattern that has large scale patterns filling the field instead of a repeated design.

Anatolian: Name applied to all Turkish rugs from the Anatolian plateau.

Aniline Dye: A type of industrial or synthetic dye derived from benzol, a product of coal tar, introduced to the carpet industry in the late nineteenth century. The dyes were not colorfast: they faded when exposed to sunlight and tended to run when damp.

Antique Finish: A chemical wash used to tone down colors and give a rug an old or antique appearance.

Aubusson: A pileless rug, generally with a floral medallion in pastel colors, once woven in France. The designs of these rugs have been adapted to pile carpets and are now woven in India and China.

Baff: Persian word for "knot."

Berdelik: Rug used as a wall hanging, often a silk rug.

Bohcha: Of Turkish origin, the word means "wrapper" and is used to describe a particular kind of bag made by folding four corners of a rug into a kind of envelope.

Bokhara: Name associated with Turkoman-design rugs woven in India and Pakistan. Also an ancient marketplace for the rugs of Turkistan.

Border: A band or series of bands surrounding the field and focal point of a carpet.

Boteh (also buta, botta): A small Oriental rug motif that resembles a shape variously described as a teardrop, pinecone, pear, or leaf, symbolizing potential growth. Because it was a defining motif of Indian wool shawls made in the paisley mills in Scotland, it is commonly known as the paisley motif.

Brocade: Weaving technique used in some flat-woven rugs whereby a supplementary weft is added into the ground warp and weft to create a pattern.

Carding: Process for preparing wool for spinning, in which two wooden paddles with metal teeth entangle the fibers so that they lie in different directions, yielding a soft, fuzzy wool.

Cartoon: A piece of graph paper on which a rug pattern has been drawn as a guide for weaving. Each square represents a single knot, the color of which is keyed to the color of the square.

Cartouche: A cloud motif that often surrounds a date or an inscription woven into a rug.

Carved Pile: Grooves cut into the rug pile to accentuate the borders and designs, done on some Chinese and Indian carpets.

Caucasian: Refers to rugs woven in the Caucasus Mountain region, a narrow strip of land between the Black and Caspian seas. These rugs are brightly colored and feature highly stylized signs.

Ceyrek: Turkish term for small rugs that measure approximately 33 by 54 inches (83 by 137cm).

Chrome Dye: A colorfast synthetic dye developed in the twentieth century and used to dye wool.

Churdjun (also Khorjun): A small saddlebag.

Chuval (also Tchuvall): In Turkoman weaving, a large storage bag usually hung from the interior framework of the Turkoman yurt, or tent.

Cicim: A type of weft-float pileless weave in which an additional wooled weft is interlaced into a rug's regular warp and weft system, giving the appearance of solid lines over the ground weave.

Closed Back: Refers to the appearance of the back of a Chinese carpet. The weft threads of a closed-back carpet are not visible because the knots completely cover them.

Cochineal: Red dye derived from the dried bodies of a species of insect.

Colorfast: Term used for a rug dye that does not change when washed or exposed to the sun.

Combing: Process for preparing wool for spinning in which wool fibers are pulled through a wooden comb with metal teeth, aligning the fibers in the same direction.

Corrosion: Deterioration of dyed fiber caused by the oxidants of a dye containing iron, often seen in dark brown or black wool.

Cut-loop Technique: Tibetan method of weaving carpets. A strand of yarn is looped around pairs of warp threads and then around a row; after a row is completed, a knife is run along the rod, cutting the pile.

Dhurrie: A pileless carpet, usually woven in India with either cotton or wool. The design is created by interweaving colored weft threads through warp threads.

DOBAG: A Turkish acronym for Natural Dye Reseach and Development Project. Rugs woven in certain cooperatives organized by provincial governments are allowed to carry the distinctive DOBAG label, which also includes the name of the weaver.

Dozar: Persian term for rugs measuring 54 by 84 inches (137 by 213cm).

Elem: Turkoman term used for the skirts of flat-woven strips at the ends of carpets. It is also applies to end panels on pile rugs replacing the earlier flat-woven strips in some Turkoman rugs. An additional panel or band woven at the top and bottom of most Turkoman rugs and bags.

Embossed Bil: Sculptured rug pile, or pile that has been trimmed or cut into a relief effect.

Ensi (also engsi or hachli, meaning "with a cross"): In Tutkoman weaving, a rug used as a doorway to the tent or dwelling.

Flat-weave: Used to describe the technique of any carpet that does not use the knotted-pile technique, including kilim, sumak, and jijim rugs.

Float: A term used to describe a portion of warp or weft threads that passes over and under two or more warp or weft threads.

Foundation: The weave of warp and weft threads of a pile rug.

Fringe: The loose ends created by the carpet's warp threads that emerge from the upper and lower ends of a rug. Sometimes the fringe is left plain; sometimes it is braided or knotted.

Ghiordes Knot (also symmetrical knot, Turkish knot): A knot in which a strand of wool encircles both warp threads with the loose ends drawn tightly between them.

Gireh: Persian word for "knot."

Gul (also gol; Persian word for "flower"): In Turkoman weaving, used to describe the characteristic repetitive small medallion. It is thought to denote the tribal affiliation of the weaver.

Hali (also Khali, kali): Term of Turkish origin, used in the Middle East as the generic word for "rug"; also the name of the most important and comprehensive magazine devoted to carpets, published in London since 1978.

Handle: A term commonly used to characterize the weight, solidity, and flexibilty of a rug. Adjectives used to describe handle include "stiff, limp, and flexible."

Hatchli: Rug design, originally Turkoman, in which the field is divided into quadrants by wide bars or strips.

Hegira (from the Arabic *Hijra*, meaning "escape or flight"): The Islamic system of recording historical dates, beginning July 16, A.D. 622, using the lunar year, which is shorter than the solar year. The calculation of equivalent dates invloves a mathematical formula.

Heybe (also Khorjin): Usually refers to a characteristic double saddlebag woven in many parts of the Middle East.

Industrial Dye (also synthetic dye, chemical dye): Dyestuff manufactured in chemical factories in Europe and later in the Middle East. Includes aniline dyes, azo dyes, and chrome dyes, all of which have been used for rug wool. All dyes are chemicals; few are traditional.

Jufti Knots (also false knots, double knots): A technique of weaving in every other hole, weakening the basic structure of the rug. In other words, the weaver uses four warp threads per knot instead of two, resulting in half the number of knots and half the amount of wool.

Kellegi: Persian term for a long, narrow rug measuring approximately 6 by 13 feet (1.8 by 4m). Also refers to the side runners in the traditional Persian layout.

Kellei: Persian term that refers to the main carpet in a traditional Persian arrangement. Usually a large rectangular carpet measuring 7 feet 6 inches by 18 feet (2.3 by 5.5m).

Kenareh: Persian term for runners measuring 2 feet 6 inches by 8 feet (0.8 by 2.4m) or 3 feet 6 inches by 20 feet (1 by 6m).

Khorjin: See **Heybe**.

Kilim: Flat-woven rugs made by using a technique in which the colored wefts that form the pattern are beaten down to cover the warps completely. Includes the common slit-tapestry technique, where vertical slits separate areas of colored weft, and other techniques where slits are avoided by interlocking wefts with one another or around a shared warp. Also, a weft-faced weave created by interweaving colored weft threads through the warp threads.

Knockout: The private auction held by members of a dealer coalition to dispose of the rugs they have bought at a public auction without bidding against one another. At the knockout, some dealers will receive rugs while others will receive money that otherwise would have gone to the original owner of the rug and auctioneeer.

Knot: The basic unit of design and structure in a pile carpet, consisting of a piece of colored wool, silk, or cotton yarn, usually looped around two warps. It produces a colored tuft of wool on the front surface of the carpet.

KSI: Knots per square inch. In the metric system, the common method of recording knot density is knots per square decimeter, or ksd, that is, knots in a square 10 centimeters on a side, containing 100 square centimeters. (To figure approximate ksd, multiply ksi by 15.5.)

Kurk Wool: The finest quality of wool used in rug weaving, consisting of the underhairs from a lamb's shoulders and flanks.

Lazy Lines: A term used to describe diagonal lines created by reversing the weft thread back on itself rather than having it carried across the width of the carpet.

Lechek (also spandrel): Persian term for the corner design of a rug.

Leckek Torunj: Persian term for a carpet designed with central and corner medallions.

Mafrash: A term of Turkish origin, it refers to the medium-size horizontal bag woven by nomadic people in various parts of the Middle East.

Mihrab: Arabic word for a niche in a mosque or community prayer hall indicating the direction of Mecca, towards which Muslims face when praying. It is also a term applied to the pointed archlike form in a sedjadeh, or prayer rug.

Mordant: A fixative used in the dyeing of wool, which enables the dye to affix to the wool.

Mosque (from the Arabic word *masjid*, meaning "place of prostration"): In the Islamic world, a building for community prayer whose floors are often covered with carpets.

Namazlyk: A term combining the Persian and Turkish words for "prayer."

Naqshe: Persian word for "pattern" or "design."

Natural Dye: A dye derived from a plant, root, flower, fruit, tree, or insect.

Node: The loop portion of the knot as it appears on the back of the rug.

Painted Rugs: Rugs designed using a system of painting the colors on with synthetic dyes.

Palas: A Caucasian kilim.

Panel Design: A rug design in which the field is divided into rectangular compartments, each of which encloses one or more motifs.

Patina: The sheen acquired by the pile of a rug with age and use.

Pile: Nap of the rug created when the knotted wool is clipped.

Programmed Rugs: A term applied to Chinese rugs indicating that the same design is "programmed" and manufactured over and over again in different sizes and colors.

Pushti: Persian term for a small pillow cover or small rug that measures 24 by 36 inches (61 by 91cm).

Roller Beam: A type of vertical loom in which warps are unrolled from a horizontal cylindrical beam at the top of the loom as the finished rug is rolled up on a smaller cylinder at the bottom. It allows for the weaving of a long run on a short loom.

Saph (Arabic word for "rank" or "row"): Applied to large carpets designed for use in mosques, with designs divided into rows of compartments, each a place for one person to pray. Also called a "family" prayer rug because the series of mihrabs, side by side, is suitable for the entire family.

Savonnerie: A rug hand-knotted in France, with a thick, heavy pile in pastel colors. Modern rugs in this design are now made in Romania.

Scoarte: A flat-weave Romanian rug woven with the slit-weave design.

Sculptured Pile: Rug pile that is embossed or clipped to give a relief effect.

Seccades: Turkish term for carpets that measure 45 by 78 inches (114 by 198cm).

Sedjadeh: (literally, "for prostration"): The Turkish word, or general term, for a rug that measures about 42 by 66 inches (107 by 168cm), suitable for one person to use for prayer. Also applied to rugs of this size with a design of the symbolic arch, doorway, or mihrab, indicating the direction of prayer—toward Mecca—or the gateway to heaven.

Selvedge: The charcteristic side finish of a rug, generally consisting of one or more warps wrapped with the ends of the wefts or with added colored wool yarns.

Senneh Knot (also symmetrical knot, Persian rug knot): A knot in which a strand of yarn encircles one warp thread and winds loosely around the other.

Shared Warp Technique: Pileless rug-weaving technique in which different-colored wefts meet and share a common warp, loop around the warp, and double back on themselves.

Slit Tapestry (also slit-weave technique, kilim): Pileless rug-weaving technique in which different-colored wefts meet and the two colors are kept separate so that each thread doubles back on itself, creating a slit at the juncture.

Stylization: The artistic process whereby an element of carpet design gradually changes over time as a result of repeated adaptations by individual weavers from the models. This usually results in gradual simplification of original forms, together with a movement away from curvilinear forms toward geometric forms.

Talim (Arabic word for "instruction"): Term used in Iran for a document written in special notation that can be read aloud as a set of knotting instructions to weavers sitting at the loom.

Traditional Dyes (also natural dyes, vegetable dyes): Dyes made and used in traditional weaving societies in the past, usually derived from plant materials such as indigo or madder root, but also made from amalgams of materials such as walnut husks and iron filing.

Turkoman: Refers to a rug from the Turkistan region. Their patterns are made of repeated guls that are unique to each tribe.

Vagireh (Persian; also wagireh): Sometimes called a "sampler," this type of small commercial rug usually woven in Iran has a variety of border and field ornaments arbitrarily woven to resemble ornaments in larger carpets.

Warp: Horizontal or vertical structural elements attached to the two end beams of a loom, upon which a rug is woven by adding weft and pile.

Weft (also woof): The widthwise or horizontal structural element of a rug, passed over and under the warps, forming part of the basic foundation of a pile rug and the design of a flat-weave rug.

Yastik (Turkish word for "cushion"): A small rug, usually woven with a knotted pile, that measures about 18 by 36 inches (46 by 91cm).

RESOURCES AND REFERENCE

The best way to learn about Oriental rugs is to do your homework. That means reading about them in books and magazines, looking at the masterpieces that are on display in most museums around the world, and studying as many rugs as you can in antique shops, department stores, and rug stores whenever and wherever you can. The sources are endless; here are just a few suggestions.

BOOKS

Bailey, Julia, and Mark Hopkins. *Through the Collecter's Eye: Oriental Rugs from New England Private Collections.* Providence, R.I.: Museum of Art, Rhode Island School of Design, 1991.

Bennett, Ian. *Oriental Carpet Identifier.* Secaucus, N.J.: Chartwell Books, Inc.,1985.

———. *Oriental Rugs.* London: Oriental Textile Press, 1980.

———, ed. *Rugs and Carpets of the World.* Edison, N.J.: The Wellfleet Press, 1977.

Bosly, Caroline. *Rugs to Riches.* New York: Pantheon Books, 1980.

Dedera, Don. *Navajo Rugs: How to Find, Evaluate, Buy, and Care for Them.* San Francisco: Northland Press, 1975.

Denny Walter B. *Oriental Rugs.* New York: Cooper-Hewitt Museum, 1979.

Dimand, Maurice, and Jean Mailey. *Oriental Rugs in the Metropolitan Museum of Art.* New York: Metropolitan Museum of Art, 1973.

Eiland, Murray L. *Oriental Rugs.* New York: New York Graphic Society, 1981.

Ellis, Charles Grant. *Oriental Carpets in the Philadelphia Museum of Art.* Philadelphia: Philadelphia Museum of Art, 1988.

Ford, P.R.J. *The Oriental Carpet.* New York: Dover Publications, Inc., 1973.

Hackmack, Adolf. *Chinese Carpets and Rugs.* New York: Dover Publications, Inc., 1973.

Hawley, Walter A. *Oriental Rugs Antique & Modern.* New York: Dover Publications, Inc., 1970.

Petsopoulos, Y. *Kilims.* New York: Rizzoli, 1979.

Summers, Janice. *The Illustrated Oriental Rugs World Buyers' Guide.* New York: Crown Publishers Inc., 1994.

Thompson, Jon. *Oriental Carpets.* New York: E.P. Duttin, 1988.

Walk in the Beauty: The Navajo and Their Blankets. New York: New York Graphic Society, 1977.

MAGAZINES AND JOURNALS

Hali, The International Journal of Oriental Carpets and Textiles. Published quarterly. Alan Marcuson, publisher and editor.

> Hali Publications Ltd.
> Kingsgate House
> Kingsgate Place
> London NW6 4TA
> England

Oriental Rug Review (ORR) and The Decorative Rug, R. O'Callaghan, editor.

Published bimonthly.
> Oriental Rug Review
> P.O. Box 709
> Meredith, NH 03253

Rug News
Published monthly.
> Museum Books Inc.
> 6 West 37th Street
> New York, NY 10018

MUSEUM COLLECTIONS

Almost every large and medium-size city throughout the world has an art museum of some sort, and many of these have a collection of interesting Oriental rugs. Collections of particular importance:

United States
The Metropolitan Museum of Art (New York City); The Museum of Fine Arts (Boston); The Textile Museum (Washington, D.C.); The Philadelphia Museum of Fine Art; The Cleveland Museum of Art; The Los Angeles County Museum of Art; The Fine Arts Museum of San Francisco; Chicago Art Institute; The Allen Art Museum (Oberlin, Ohio); Museum of the American Indian (New York); The Denver Art Museum.

Europe
The Victoria and Albert Museum (London); The Museum of Decorative Arts (Paris); Museum of Applied Arts (Vienna); Poldi Pezzoli Museum (Milan); Rijksmuseum (Amsterdam); Berlin Museums (Berlin).

Middle East
Museum of Turkish and Islamic Art and Museum of Pious Foundations (Istanbul); Carpet Museum of Teheran; Kuwait National Museum (Kuwait City); Museum of Islamic Arts (Cairo).

PHOTOGRAPHY CREDITS

INDEX